Lures, Flies and Baits

for Freshwater Fish

OUTDOOR LIFE TAKE-ALONG BOOKS

Lures, Flies and Baits

for Freshwater Fish

F. Philip Rice

Drawings by Charles Berger

OUTDOOR LIFE • HARPER & ROW

NEW YORK • LONDON

Library of Congress Catalog Card No.: 70-153430

Designed by Jeff Fitschen

Manufactured in the United States of America

CONTENTS

Part IV—RECOMMENDATIONS FOR DIFFERENT FISHES

INTRODUCTION

This book is divided into four Parts:

Part I—Lures
Part II—Flies
Part III—Baits
Part IV—Recommendations For Different Fishes

In the first three Parts, the author has described and categorized the enormous variety of lures, flies, and baits used today by American fishermen. The main *types* of lures are shown in photographs, with captions that identify the lure, tell for which fish it is designed, and how it is meant to be fished. Drawings show the main types of flies and the various types of bait. The purpose of these three Parts is to give the reader a detailed knowledge of this vast—sometimes confusing—subject so that he will be able to distinguish between one lure (or fly) and the next according to his needs; also, that he will be more aware of the many options available to him in fishing bait.

Part IV consists of specific recommendations for every important freshwater gamefish. In compiling this material, the author queried fish and game departments in every state, noted fishermen, and tackle manufacturers. The suggestions therefore represent a broad segment of angling opinion and include regional favorites from all over the country.

Of course, there is no *one* lure, fly, or bait which is "best" for a particular fish. If there were, fishing would not be the challenge that it is. But it is hoped that the angler will use the suggestions in this book to build a better lure and fly collection. In addition, the book will serve as a handy reference on lake or stream when the problem of "no hits" may seem insoluble. For only by experimenting can the fisherman discover what the fish are taking that day.

Finally, by delving deeper into the subject of lures, flies, and baits, the reader will gain a better understanding of fish behavior and perhaps edge closer to solving the baffling problem of how to tease a fish into striking—the problem that sends anglers back to try again and again.

PART II

Lures

SURFACE LURES

Bobber Lures. These are bobbers with hooks attached; they are used plain, or with bait attached, either on the surface or anchored off the bottom of the stream or river with a dropper weight holding them down. Some types are called "cherry bobbers" and are a favorite for steelheads in the Pacific Northwest.

Plunkers, Poppers, Chuggers. These lures have concave faces which splash water when the lure is jerked, making a loud plunking, popping, chugging noise.

Stick Lures. These long, slim lures float vertically in the water, tail down. The head bobs down and the tail goes up when the lure is jerked. Stick lures have plenty of action while remaining in one place, allowing the fisherman to fish good spots thoroughly.

Sputterers. These lures kick up the surface of the water when retrieved, usually with spinning propellers.

Swimming Animal Lures. These lures do not necessarily look like animals, although they may, but they kick up a fuss on the water as they are swimming, thus imitating an animal struggling.

Torpedo Lures. These are thicker versions of stick lures. Like stick lures, they do not have any spinners or diving bills, but float horizontally in the water. All action must be imparted by the fisherman.

Wounded Minnow Lures. These imitations of fish or minnows float horizontally on the water and always have propeller spinners fore or aft, or both places, and are designed to represent a dying fish struggling on the water surface.

Surface Lures

a. CHUGGER SPOOK. Rests on water at slant, makes splashing, popping sound when jerked. An old-timer, very effective for bass.

b. HULA POPPER. Hollow face makes loud popping, splashing sound when lure is retrieved. Rubber skirt imparts enticing action. One of the most effective bass lures.

c. SPUTTERBUG. Head spinner creates surface commotion when lure is reeled fast. Slow retrieve gives paddling sound. Good for bass, pickerel.

d. CRAZY CRAWLER. Swimming animal lure with crawling action; two arms paddle the water. Small size good for bass, large for musky.

e. DYLITE SPINNING FROG. Swimming animal lure for bass or pickerel. Cast onto bank or lily pad and hop it into the water like a frog.

a
b
c

d
e

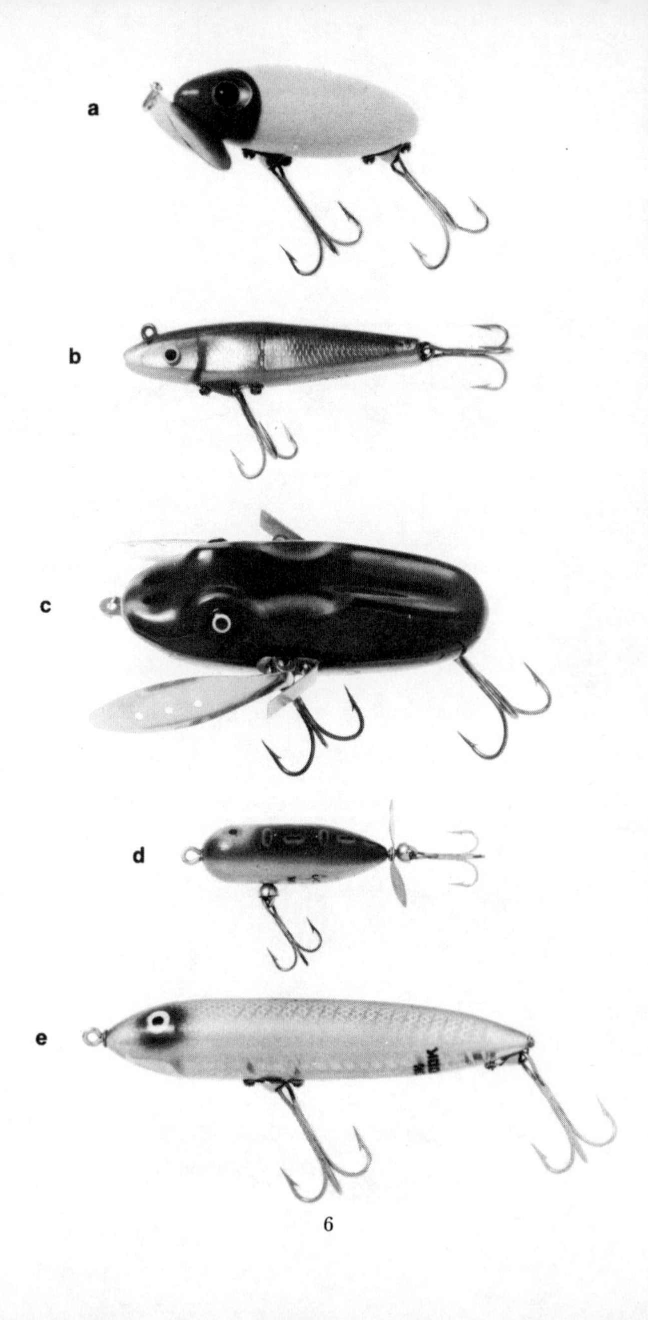
a
b
c
d
e

Surface Lures

a. JITTERBUG. Swimming animal lure with gurgling side-to-side action when retrieved. One of the most effective lures for largemouth and smallmouth; also good for pickerel, musky.

b. MIRROLURE. Torpedo lure which floats on top, runs below surface when retrieved. Effective for bass, pickerel, pike, musky.

c. LEBOEUF CREEPER. Swimming animal lure with a paddling, creeping action. Good for largemouth, smallmouth, pickerel, musky.

d. TINY TORPEDO. Wounded minnow lure with propeller on tail. Effective for bass, pickerel, and in large models, for musky.

e. ZARA SPOOK. Torpedo lure which darts, dives, veers when rod tip is jerked. Old-timer for bass, pike, pickerel, musky.

FLOATING-DIVING PLUGS

Darters. A V-shaped face gives these plugs a darting motion when retrieved. They float on top and run quite shallow when moving.

Deep Divers. A large diving bill enables these lures to dive up to 12–15 feet deep when retrieved.

Vibrators. A deep, flat body gives these lures a fast wiggle or vibration as they move through the water, emitting sonic waves in the water to attract the fish.

Wobblers. These lures usually run quite shallow with a pronounced side-to-side wobble. They come in various shapes and sizes: banana shaped, like a Flatfish; long and slim, like a Rapala; sausage shaped, like a Bass-Oreno; minnow shaped, like a River Runt.

SINKING PLUGS

Deep Divers. Not only do these plugs sink, but a large diving bill enables them to dive down quite deep when retrieved. They are of various shapes; sometimes long and slim, other times short and fat.

Vibrators. With the hook eye near the top of the body, and a deep, flat body, these lures are made to vibrate very fast, giving off sound waves in the water to attract fish.

Sinking Wobblers. They sink, they wobble, they catch lots of fish.

SPOONS

Spoons come in many different sizes, shapes, finishes, and actions. Generally, they might be divided into two broad categories: *casting or trolling spoons* and *jigging spoons.* However, it's hard to classify them in this way because many jigging spoons may be cast or trolled and any casting or trolling spoon may be jigged.

Generally, the broader the spoon, the easier it wobbles with a slow retrieve, and the shallower it runs. A long, slim spoon usually darts, swims, and flutters. Also, a spoon made of light metal will run shallow, while one of heavy metal for the same size and shape will run quite deep.

Some spoons will spin when retrieved too rapidly, causing line twist, so have to be used with rudders or a lot of swivels. Others require a very fast retrieve to bring out the best action. The fisherman ought to observe the spoon while retrieving to determine the optimum speed to bring out the best action.

See following pages for photos of floating-diving plugs, sinking plugs, spoons, spinners, bugs, and poppers.

Floating-Diving Plugs

a. CREEK CHUB DARTER. Shallow-running plug that darts erratically from side to side. Effective for warm-water gamefish when they're feeding in the shallows.

b. BOMBER. Floating plug that dives deep on retrieve. The larger the plug, the deeper it dives. Excellent deep-water bass lure, for casting or trolling. Also good for walleyes, pickerel, pike.

c. REBEL SHINER. Floats at rest, dives deep and wobbles when retrieved. For all warm-water gamefish when they are deep; can be trolled for salmon.

d. THINFIN SILVER SHAD. Floater-diver with wobbling, darting action. For all warm-water fish.

e. CREEK CHUB PIKIE. Dives and wobbles from side to side when retrieved. An old-timer, one of the best all-round plugs for warm-water gamefish.

f. FLATFISH. Dives and swims with a violent, rapid, side-to-side wiggle. Good for all species of gamefish: small sizes for panfish, trout; medium sizes for bass, pickerel, walleyes, small pike; larger sizes for pike, musky, lake trout, salmon.

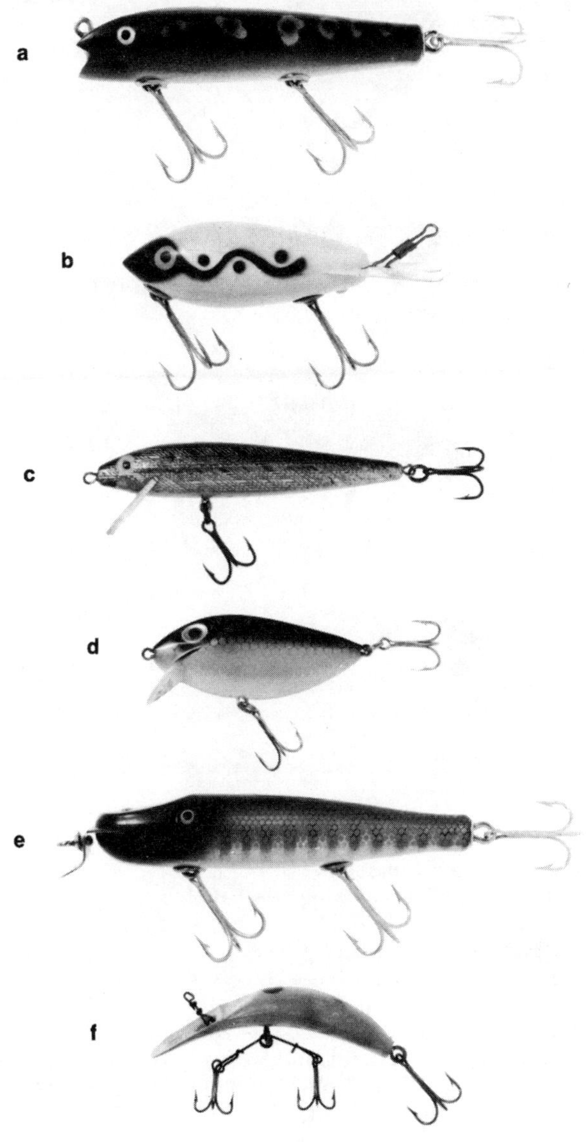
a
b
c
d
e
f

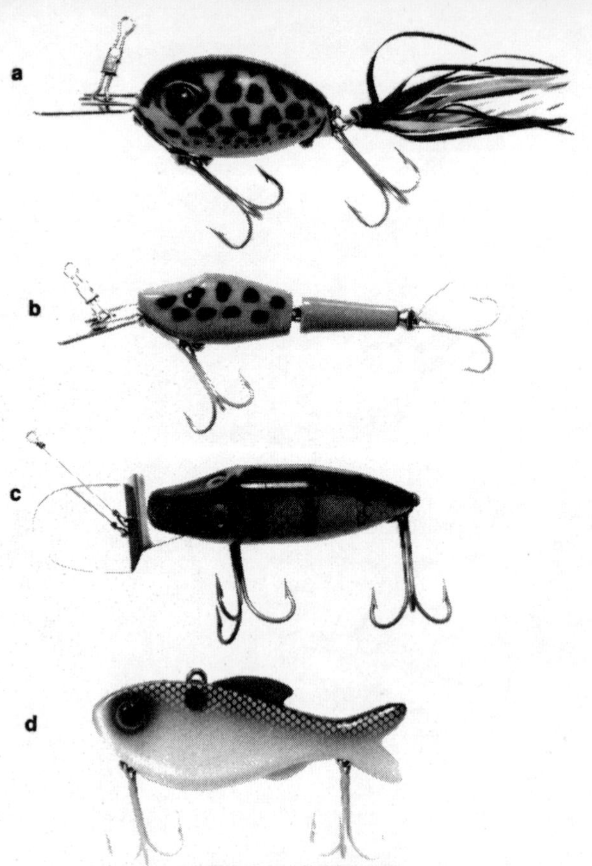

Sinking Plugs

a. ARBOGASTER. Deep-running lure with a fast wiggle, primarily for bass.

b. HULA PIKIE. Sinking, deep-diving plug; jointed body gives it a side-to-side wiggle. Good for bass, pike, walleyes, pickerel in deep water.

c. RIVER RUNT. Sinks slowly, dives deep on retrieve. Faster the retrieve, the deeper it dives. Favorite deep-water lure for bass, walleyes, pike, pickerel.

d. TRU-SHAD. Vibrating lure with a fast wiggle. Smaller sizes are for medium depth, larger for deep running. A fine lure for bass, walleyes, pike.

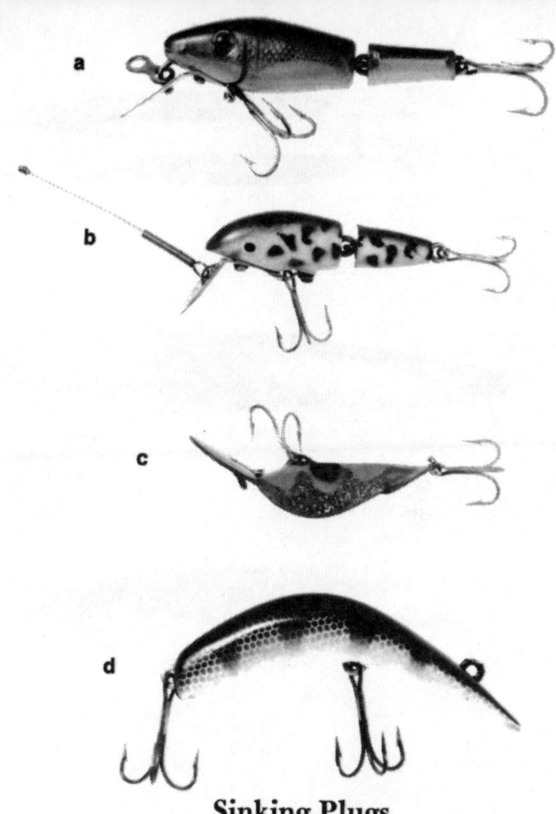

Sinking Plugs

a. MIRROLURE. Wobbling lure designed to sink and dive on the retrieve. Small sizes good for perch, crappie, white and yellow bass, rock bass, white perch.

b. CISCO KID. Rapidly sinking plug that dives deeper on the retrieve. Useful for deep walleyes, bass.

c. SPOONPLUG. Wobbling lure that runs deep, especially good for bottom-bumping for bass in deep water.

d. LAZY IKE. Banana-shaped wobbler that swims with a rapid wiggle, best when retrieved slowly. Effective for bass, panfish, trout, salmon in appropriate sizes.

a

b

c

d

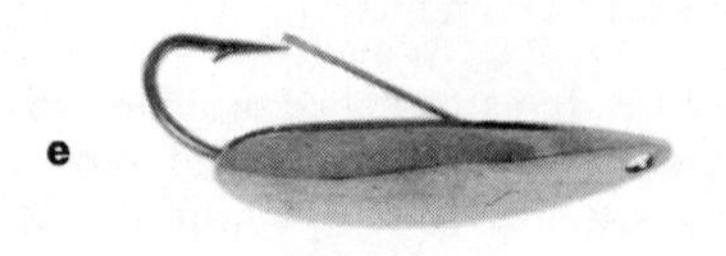
e

Spoons

a. COP-E-CAT. Wobbling spoon, a large version of the Dardevle. Tops for large salmon, pike, musky, sea-run trout.

b. ABU-TOBY. Fins give this spoon a darting action. Useful for trout, salmon, warm-water gamefish.

c. ABU-KOSTAR. Most often used as a trolling spoon because of its heavy weight. Excellent for large anadromous trout, salmon, lake trout. Also pike, musky.

d. RED EYE WIGGLER. Wobbling spoon that may be retrieved slowly or fast and still have fine action. Large sizes good for pike, musky, bass, pickerel, lake trout; small sizes for trout.

e. JOHNSON'S SILVER MINNOW. Wobbling spoon with a swimming action. Does not revolve. Single, weedless hook. Well-earned reputation for catching warm-water gamefish in weeds, stumps, brush, usually with pork rind added. Also used for trout and coho salmon.

Spoons

a. MR. CHAMP. Wobbling spoon which doesn't spin and twist line. May be used for casting, jigging, trolling. Popular for warm-water fish, panfish, trout, salmon.

b. LIMPER. Darting, shallow-running spoon that doesn't twist. Good for panfish, trout, warm-water gamefish, salmon. Made with single hook in 9 sizes for coho salmon.

c. AL'S GOLDFISH. Wobbling spoon, most effective at slow speeds. One of the best for trout and salmon, but also good for warm-water gamefish.

d. TONY ACCETTA PET. Darting spoon with a slight wobble. Comes in weedless and standard models. Pork strip or chunk gives added attraction for bass. Also used for trout, salmon, panfish, and larger warm-water gamefish in appropriate sizes.

e. SIDEWINDER. Wobbling spoon with a fluttering, side-to-side action which won't twist line. Excellent in fast water. Good for all gamefish.

f. PHANTOM WOBBLER. Wobbling spoon that won't twist line unless retrieved too fast. One of the best for trout and salmon; very popular in New England.

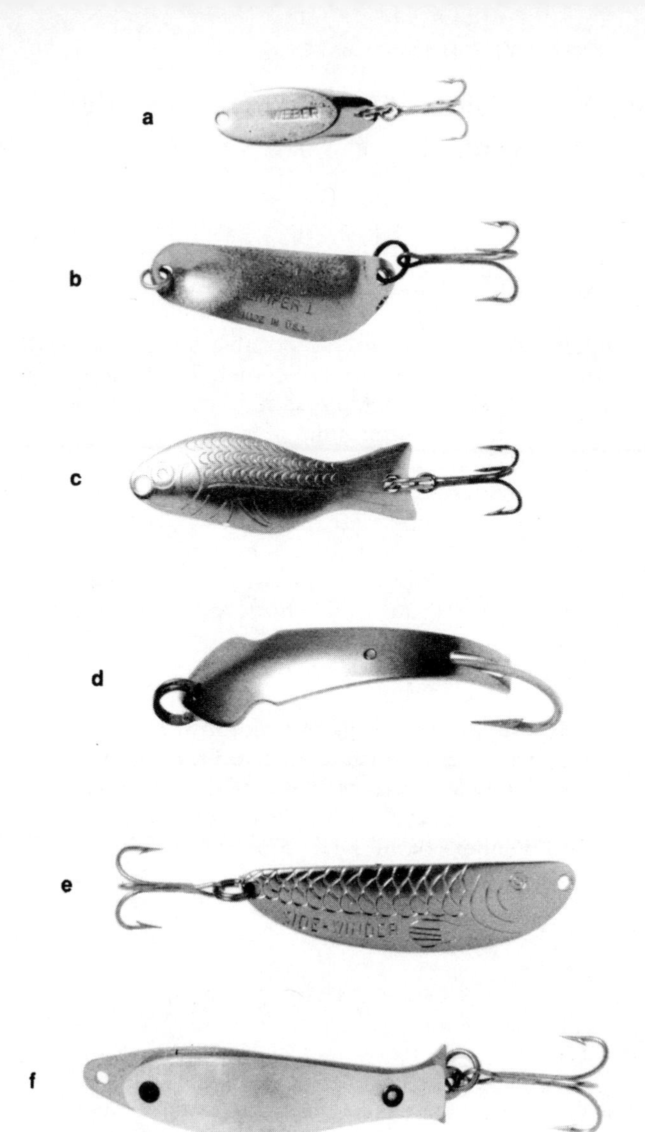
a
b
c
d
e
SIDE-WINDER
f

SPINNERS, WEIGHTED SPINNERS, SPINNER COMBINATIONS

Plain spinners can be classified according to blade design and shape. Blades which are short and round, like the *Colorado Spinner,* have the greatest resistance in the water so spin the easiest with the slowest retrieve. Sometimes these spinners have too much resistance so are impossible to use in fast currents. They spin at a wide angle from the shaft. Blades which are long and slim, like the *Willowleaf Spinner,* have a minimum of resistance and spin fast and close to the shaft. They require a faster retrieve or faster water to make them spin.

Of course, spinners are often used in conjunction with a lure, fly, or bait, either weighted or unweighted. The spinner attracts the fish, which then bites the lure. Sometimes, however, a spinner attached to a weighted body with a bare treble hook is a wonderful fish catcher.

Trolling Spinner Rigs. A series of spinners made up on wire shafts, with attractive beads, of various graded sizes and shapes, are used as attractors for trolling. They are called "Christmas Trees" or "Ford Fenders" and by a number of other nicknames.

SAFETY-PIN LURES

Safety-pin lures are so named because they have a V-shaped, stainless-steel wire shaft the shape of half a safety pin offset from the main body of the lure. The shaft holds a jig spinner or two. The entire lure is really a jig or other lure to which a jig spinner has been added. It is extremely versatile and can be fished shallow or deep. Some come in weedless models and can be fished through weedbeds or over and around rocks, stumps, and brush. Most are used as jigging lures off or near the bottom.

JIGS, JIG COMBINATIONS

Jig heads come in a variety of sizes and shapes. They vary in weight from 1/64 ounce to 6 ounces or more (for use in salt water). Jig heads may be purchased which are molded around a single plain hook. The hook may be baited with live bait, cut bait, plastic worm, eel, or pork rind or other attractor.

However, some jigs come with a skirt attached. The most commonly used skirts are hair (bucktail, polar bear hair, squirrel tail hair, skunk, etc.), feathered streamers, Maribou, nylon, rubber, plastic, or yarn.

Since jigs are often used on or near the bottom, the design is important to prevent snags. The hook should ride up and the head should be of a shape to allow it to bump over rocks or logs. Some jigs seem to snag continually; others ride successfully over most obstacles. Of course, if the jig is used near the surface, when larger fish are feeding on baitfish, a flat design (such as the coin shape) will keep the jig near the surface. Or, a slanted head may be used successfully since the fisherman does not have to worry about snagging, as he would if he were fishing this same jig near the bottom. Of course, many jigs come with weedless hooks and these help prevent snagging. It is important that the hook be kept sharp since it is often difficult to hook a fish which is in quite deep water.

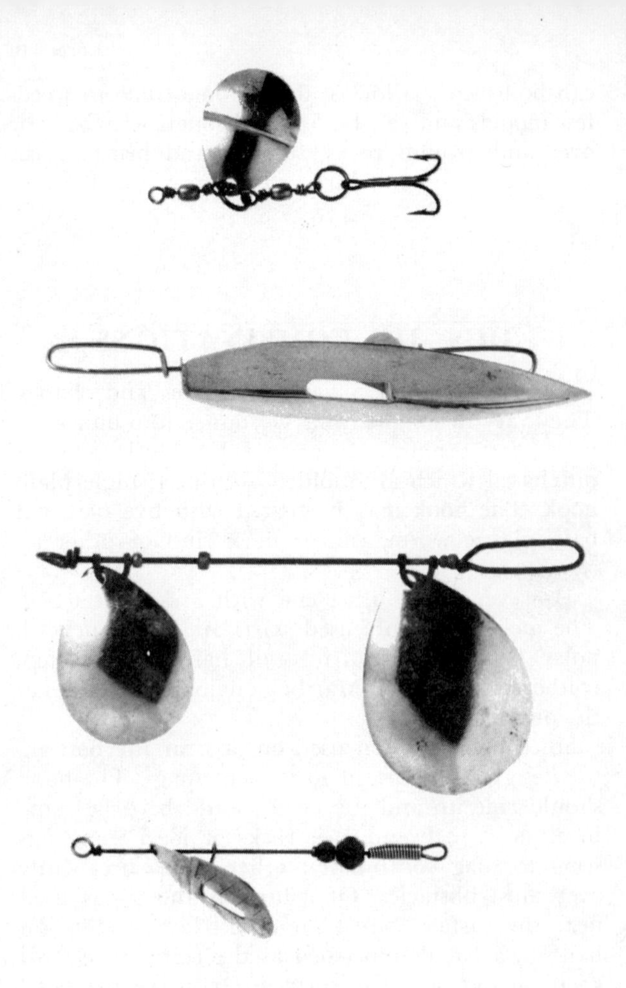

Four basic types of spinners (*from top*): Colorado Spinner; Willow Leaf Spinner; Indiana Spinner; June Bug Spinner.

Two weedless spinning lures: Shimmy Wiggler (*top*) and Hawaiian Wiggler. Both are good for bass, walleyes, pike, and pickerel.

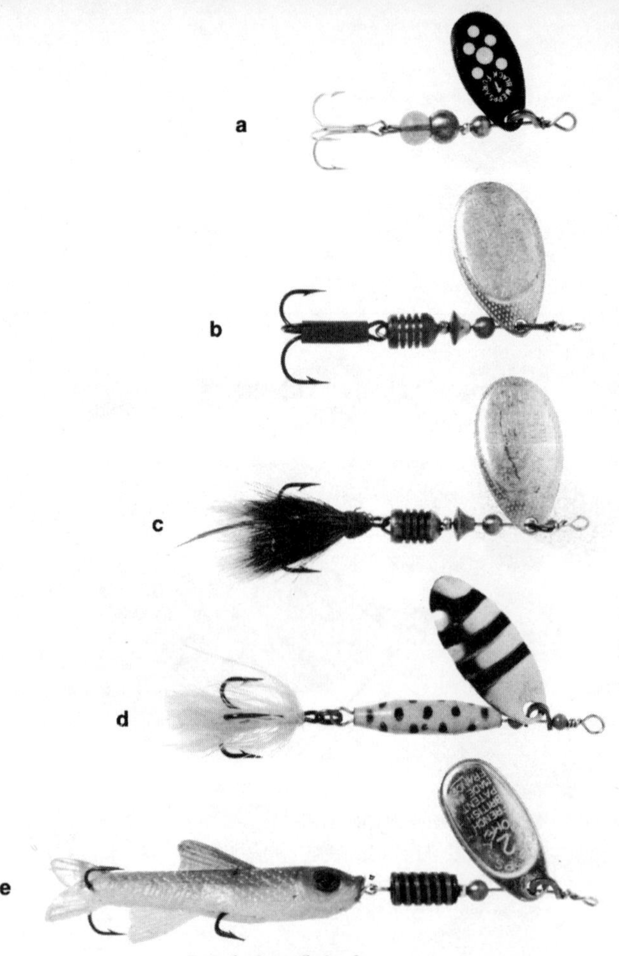

Weighted Spinners

a. MEPPS BLACK FURY

b. MEPPS AGLIA PLAIN

c. MEPPS AGLIA WITH SQUIRREL TAIL

d. ABU REFLEX

e. MEPPS AGLIA COMET WITH MINNOW

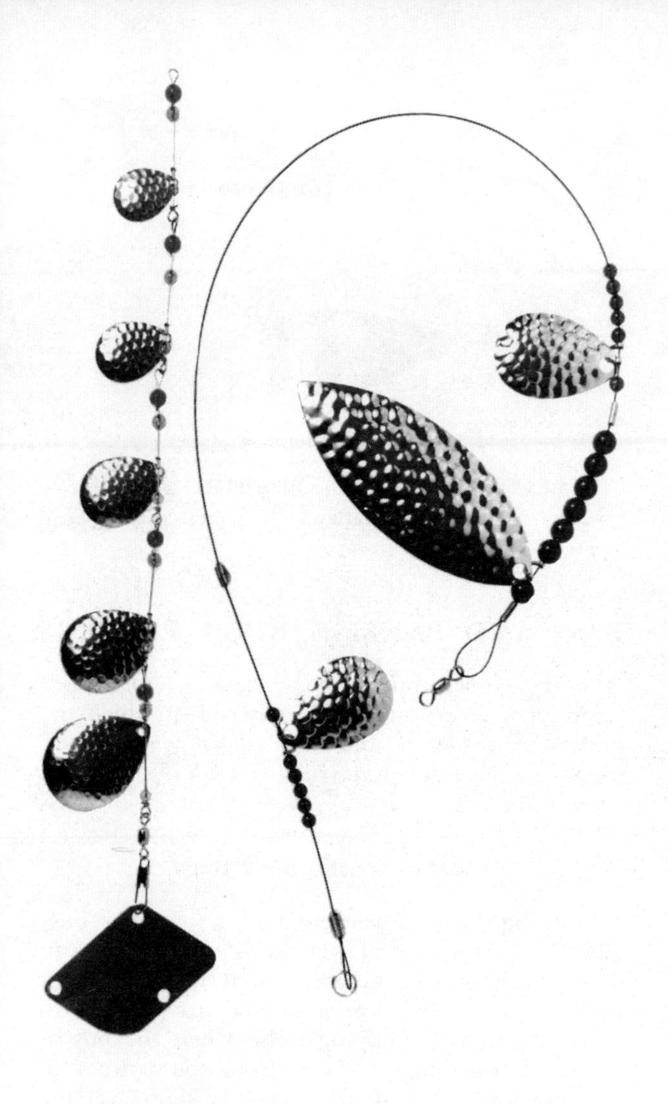

Typical trolling rigs for lake trout and other deep-running gamefish: the Webertroll (*left*) and the Dave Davis Spinner.

Typical safety-pin lure, the Busy Body, is good for deep-water bass and walleyes.

BASS AND PANFISH BUGS, POPPERS

Bass and panfish bugs may be classified into three basic types according to the material of which the bodies are made: (1) those with *hard bodies* (*cork, plastic*); (2) those of *deer hair;* and (3) those of *sponge rubber.*

Cork or Plastic Body Bugs

Popping Bugs. The design of a popping bug, whether of cork or of plastic, is very important. The bug has to be buoyant, so it will float high in the water. The face should be scooped out to make a gurgling, popping noise when the bug is jerked, but it should slope (from the bottom to the top) forward, so it will plane or skim over the water easily without diving on the pickup. The hook should stick out far enough from the body of the bug to allow easy hooking of the fish. The skirt, tail, wings, or legs should be durable (whether of hackle, feather, rubber or plastic) and strongly attached.

Torpedo-Head Bugs. The torpedo-head bug was one of the earliest designs. Actually, it must represent a swimming minnow on the water surface. The buoyant head skims over the top of the water, the hackle and feathers vibrate and wave.

Slim Bugs. These bugs have a reversed bullet-shaped body, but are quite long and slim. Usually do not have a concave face to give a popping noise. Look like large water spiders with plastic or cork bodies.

Frogs. These are really popping bugs but with finishes and designs to imitate frogs.

Mice. The majority of mice imitations are made of deer hair (see the section on deer-hair bugs), but there is one plastic model which deserves special mention, the Dylite Weedless Fly Rod Mouse.

Rubber Legs. The addition of rubber legs to popping bugs or other types of bugs adds considerably to their attractiveness. A number of bugs come with or without rubber legs.

Weedless Bugs. Several models of bugs already discussed come in weedless models.

Deer-Hair Bugs

Deer-hair bugs are useful when the fish do not seem to want a hard-bodied, noisy lure (such as a plastic or cork popping bug). The deer hair gives maximum buoyancy (although not as good as light

a
b
c
d

e

Bass and Panfish Bugs

a. FLY ROD POPPER. Highly effective for bass.

b. FIREBUG. Torpedo-head bug with phosphorescent plastic body and tail-strip, feather tail. Used for bass, especially at night.

c. DYLITE POPPING FROG. High-floating popper for bass.

d. DYLITE NITWIT. Slim bug for panfish.

e. DYLITE SLIM BUG. For bass, panfish.

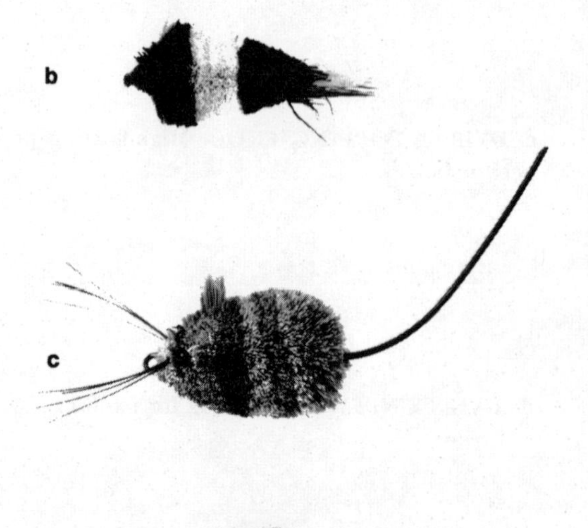

d

Bass and Panfish Bugs

a. HAIR BUG. Deer-hair bug for bass.

b. HENSHALL LURE. Deer-hair bug for bass.

c. HAIR MOUSE. Effective for bass, pickerel, pike.

d. MOUNTAIN HOPPER. Deer-hair lure for panfish, also good for trout.

plastic or cork), but the main advantage is the life-like appearance which the deer hair creates. Many anglers prefer deer-hair bugs, especially under calm, quiet-water conditions, to the hard-bodied types. A well-equipped angler ought to have both types.

Henshall-Type Lures. These are named after Dr. James A. Henshall, a noted angler-author of the last century. These bugs have clipped deer-hair bodies, outstretched wings, and hair and hackle tails. They represent any type of moth, dragon fly, etc. floating on the water with wings out.

Sponge Rubber Bugs

Spiders and hoppers in sponge rubber are sometimes designed to float, at other times to sink. They are used extensively and very successfully on bluegill and other sunfish. In fact, a number of fishermen would say they are the best lure for bluegills. They are used a much less extent on trout.

PART II

Flies

DRY FLIES

Dry flies, especially for trout, have been divided traditionally into eleven groups:

Bivisibles
Divided wing
Downwing
Fanwing
Hackle
Hairbody
Hairwing
Midge
Spentwing
Spider
Variant

Three additional newer types of flies ought to be added to this list: *gauze wing, keel flies,* and *parachute flies.* The *gauze wing* is most often made of just that: gauze (sometimes plastic), while the *keel fly* is so named because it is tied on a special type of keel hook that rides upright, thus preventing snagging. The *parachute fly* is tied so the hackle rides horizontally in the plane of water. The wings are sometimes hair, at other times feathers.

A *bivisible* is a hackle fly without wings, with a lighter color of hackle in front, thus increasing the visibility of the fly while on the water.

A *divided-wing* fly is the standard dry fly with erect wings, a hackle collar, and body and tail of various materials.

A *downwing* fly has wings which lie back along the body. Other parts of the fly are made of various materials.

A *fanwing* has large, flat wings which protrude at an upward and outward angle from the hook shank.

A *hackle* fly is tied without wings. It may be all hackle (Palmer style), or have fairly heavy hackle on the collar in front of a body and tail.

A *hairbody* fly has a clipped deer hair body which gives it great buoyancy in the water.

A *hairwing* fly has hair wings of bucktail, squirrel tail, or similar hair tied to stand erect. The body, tail, and hackle may be similar to a divided-wing fly.

A *midge* is actually any fly of extremely small size, often tied on #20, #22, or as small as #28 hook.

A *spentwing* fly has wings which protrude horizontally from the body of the fly. It is not often used today.

A *spider* type of fly has wingless, extra-long hackles, and a very light hook to make the fly float high and dry on the surface.

A *variant* is tied with extra-long hackles (like a spider) but with small wings added. Like the spider, it floats high on the water, resembling an insect hovering on or over the water.

There are a number of subdivisions of flies under some of these categories, but these specialized types will be discussed when patterns are discussed. A special group of flies (some of which are fished dry) known as *terrestrials,* because they imitate insects which hatch on land and fall in the water, are discussed in a separate section.

In gathering information on commonly used dry-fly patterns, the author queried fish and game departments of all fifty states, along with numerous sportsmen and outdoor writers around the country. These suggestions, plus the wealth of information in the angling literature, plus the author's own experience have enabled him to condense a dry-fly list down to workable size and still include the most commonly used patterns across the United States and Canada. These patterns have been developed primarily for trout, although they will catch, and

BASIC TYPES OF DRY FLIES

SPIDER

DOWNWING

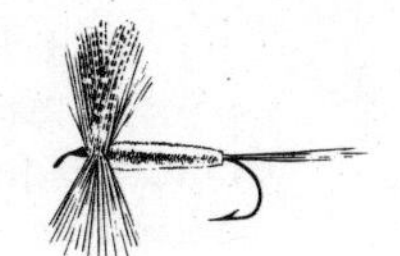

DIVIDED WING

VARIANT

HACKLE

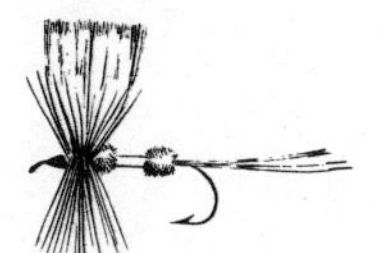

FANWING

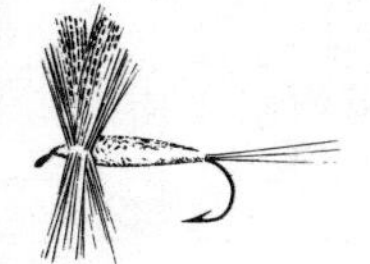

HAIRBODY

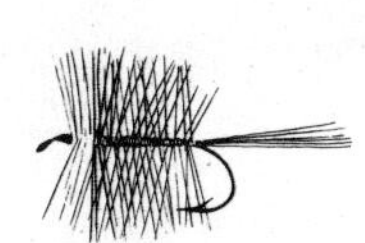

BIVISIBLE

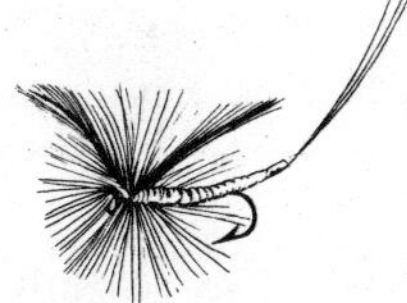

SPENTWING

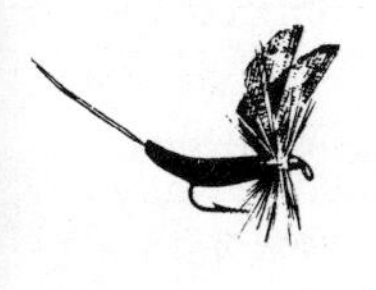

GAUZE WING

KEEL FLY

PARACHUTE FLY

TYPES OF HAIRWINGS

HAIRWING

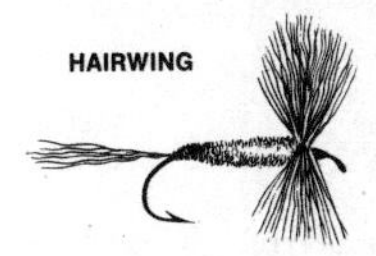

TRUDE FLY

CADDIS FLY

BIRD'S STONEFLY

are used for, many other fish: salmon, bass, and panfish especially. However, flies which were specifically designed for salmon and steelhead are discussed in a separate chapter.

Bivisible Patterns

Badger	Ginger
Black	Gray
Blue Dun	Grizzly
** Brown	

Sizes 10, 12, 14, 16 are most common.

Divided Wing Patterns

** Adams or Female Adams
** Black Gnat
** Blue Dun
* Blue Quill
Cahill, Dark
** Cahill, Light
* Coachman (more often used wet)
** Ginger Quill
** Hendrickson (dark or light)
* Iron Blue Dun
March Brown
McGinty (more often used wet)
** Mosquito
Olive Dun (dark or light)
Olive Quill (dark or light)
Pink Lady
** Quill Gordon
Red Quill
* Rio Grande King (a western fly, many times used wet)
** Royal Coachman
White Miller

Sizes 10, 12, 14, 16 are most common.

** Most frequently mentioned
* Very frequently mentioned

Downwing Patterns

The most famous downwing patterns are the *Muddler Minnow, Hopper Fly* and *Hornberg Special.* Please see the section on Streamer Flies for a discussion of the Muddler Minnow and the section on Terrestrials for a discussion of the Hopper Fly and Hornberg Special.

Fanwing Patterns

Ginger Quill
Light Cahill
Quill Gordon
** Royal Coachman

Sizes 8, 10, 12, 14 are most common.

Hackle Patterns

** Brown Hackle, Peacock
Brown Hackle, Yellow
Gray Hackle, Peacock
Gray Hackle, Red
** Gray Hackle, Yellow
Tups Indispensable

Sizes 10, 12, 14, 16 are most common.

Hairbody Patterns

** Deer Hair Fly (the original Irresistible)
Goofus Bug
Humdinger
Humpy
** Irresistible

See sections on Bass and Panfish Bugs and on Terrestrials for additional hairbody flies.

Hairwing Patterns

There are a number of subdivisions of hairwing dry flies. These include: *Wulff Flies, Trude Flies, Caddis Flies, Stone Flies,* and *Standard Hairwing Patterns.*

Wulff Flies

Black
Blonde
* Brown
** Gray
Grizzly
* Royal
White

Sizes 8, 10, 12, 14 are most common.

** Most frequently mentioned
* Very frequently mentioned

Trude Flies

Grizzly King	Red Trude
O'Connor Rio Grande King	Royal Coachman

Sizes 6, 8, 10, 12
May be fished dry or wet.

Caddis Flies

Bucktail Caddis	Kolzer Firefly
Sizes 6, 8, 10, 12	Sizes 8, 10, 12, 14

Stone Flies

Bird's Stone Fly, Sizes 4, 6, 8, 10, 3X long shank
Sofa Pillow, Sizes 4, 6, 8, 10, 2X long shank

Standard Hairwing Patterns

Many different dry fly patterns may be obtained with hair wings. The most common is:

** Hairwing Royal Coachman

Midges

The term generally refers to any fly in extremely small sizes, #20, 22, and even as small as 28. The following midge patterns are tied by the Orvis Company, Manchester, Vermont.

Adams Midge (#20, 22)	Cream Midge (#20, 22)
Black Midge (#20, 22, 28)	Ginger Midge (#28)
Blue Dun Midge (#20, 22)	Olive Midge (#20, 22)
Brown Midge (#20, 22)	

In addition, the following dry-fly patterns are tied by Orvis as small as #20: Black Gnat, Dark Cahill, Dark Hendrickson, Female Adams, Ginger Quill, Light Cahill, Mosquito, Quill Gordon, and Royal Coachman.

The following midges are tied by Hank Roberts, size #18, 20: Gray Midge, Mosquito, Black Midge, Blue Quill Midge, Ginger Quill Midge.

Spentwing Patterns

Standard dry-fly patterns are sometimes still tied in spentwing style. Generally this style has been discontinued by most tiers. One special fly, the Dragon Fly, deserves mention.

Spider Patterns

Considered one of the finest dry flies because of superior floating qualities. Most common patterns include:

Badger	** Brown
Black	Furnace
* Blue Dun	** Ginger

Variant Patterns

Badger	Ginger
Blue	* Multi-colored Variant
* Brown	** Red Variant

Gauze Wing Patterns

Dragonfly, Sizes 4, 6, 8, 10, 12
Gauze Wing Drake, Sizes 10, 12
Lifelike May Fly, Sizes 8, 10, 12
May Fly, Sizes 8, 10, 12, 14
Natural Drake Flies, Sizes 8, 10

Keel Fly Patterns

Keel Fly Dries, Sizes 12, 14, 16

** Most frequently mentioned
* Very frequently mentioned

Parachute Fly Patterns

Adams	Pale Evening Dun
Beaverkill	Parmacheene Belle
* Black Gnat	Professor
Blue Dun	Rio Grande King
* Cahill, Dark	* Royal Coachman
* Cahill, Light	Silver Doctor
Coachman	White Miller
Gray Hackle, Peacock	Yellow May
McGinty	

* Very frequently mentioned

There are dozens of local fly tiers across the country, but the following large companies ought to be able to supply most of the patterns of dry flies you need (see Appendix for complete addresses).

Dan Bailey's Fly Shop
Glen Evans
Hank Roberts Outfitters
Keel Fly Company (Keel Flies only)
M. Behrens
The Orvis Co.
Phillips Fly and Tackle Co. (Tie only special types: deer hair flies, Wulff flies, gauze wing)
Weber Tackle
Worth Fishing Tackle

WET FLIES

Traditionally, wet flies for trout have been grouped into four major categories: *divided wing, feather wing, hackle,* and *hairwing.*

The *divided-wing* fly (tied wet) has wings made from carefully paired quill feathers with their concave side facing outward. The wings are usually bent back slightly over the body (in contrast to dry flies that have wings tied fairly upright). Also, the wet fly has a fairly heavy hook to sink the fly, a body which sinks instead of floats, and hackle which is less carefully selected than that for dry flies (usually the hackle on wet flies is more limber and has more webbing). Of course, any divided-wing fly (tied dry) may also be fished wet by submerging the fly, or divided-wing flies may be purchased which are labeled wet and dry, but it's usually better to select wet flies which are specifically designed to sink.

The *featherwing* fly is made from speckled flank, side, and breast feathers of various ducks. These feathers are not as stiff as the divided-wing flies, but are more durable and look more lifelike.

The *hackle* fly is probably the most durable of all and is dressed without wings, with hackle at the shoulders in front of the body, or Palmer style over the whole body (in place of any body sometimes).

The *hairwing* fly utilizes hair from bucktails, squirrel tails, or from other animals for the wings.

Today, there are other wet trout flies made of materials which make it hard to classify them into any of the above four categories. For example, some new types of flies have gauze wings, others have sponge-rubber bodies, others have rubber feelers for legs, or a combination of material. One new type of fly, the *keel fly,* is named because it is tied on a special hook which rides upright in the water. Therefore, the following categories of wet flies might be added to the traditional four groups: *gauze wing, rubber body or legs,* and *keel flies.*

What about flies which are designated panfish flies, "brim" flies, crappie flies, or bass spinner flies? Actually, these may be variations of flies in one or more of the four traditional wet trout fly groups, or they may be flies which do not at all fit into any of the traditional categories. For example, a panfish fly, or "brim" fly, usually is a hackle fly with a chenille body, or an all-hackle fly tied in colors that do not always follow traditional patterns. A bass spinner fly is usually a large version of a traditional pattern of trout fly (the pattern is not always faithfully followed) but with upright and flat (not divided) wings. Therefore, for want of a better system, two other categories have been designated and these are *panfish flies* and *bass spinner flies.* Of course, panfish and bass are both caught on trout flies of any type, or they may be caught on bugs designed specially for them, so not all panfish and bass flies are grouped into just two categories, but these two categories are nearly always used to designate the off-beat flies described above (hackle flies or winged flies made especially for panfish, and large flatwing flies, often fished with spinners, made especially for bass).

There are still other flies labeled *salmon flies* or *steelhead flies.* These are usually tied wet with sparse dressing and extra-heavy hooks so the flies will sink readily, but there are some which are tied dry or streamer style. All get their designation from the fact that they are tied especially for Atlantic salmon (very few are designed specifically for Pacific salmon) or for steelhead trout (sea-run rainbows). However, since they are not trout flies, they will be discussed in a section for them.

This leaves nine catergories of wet flies:

Divided wing
Featherwing
Hackle
Hairwing
Gauze wing
Rubber body or legs
Keel flies
Panfish flies
Bass spinner flies

There are thousands of patterns of wet flies. Which ones should the fisherman buy? Out of the thousands of patterns, several dozens are used most frequently throughout the United States and Canada. The patterns suggested in this chapter do not include all of the good wet flies (all flies will catch fish at some time or other), but they do include a majority of those which are used and suggested most frequently. The final selections have been made after corresponding with fish and game departments, outdoor writers, and fishermen all over the United States.

A fisherman should keep in mind that it is important to select types, and sizes, as well as patterns, so the patterns have been grouped into nine categories to make it easier for the fisherman to select from each type.

BASIC TYPES OF WET FLIES

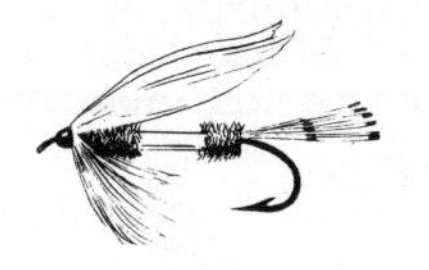

DIVIDED WING

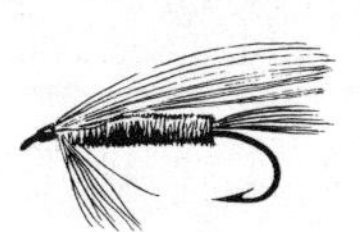

HAIRWING

FEATHERWING

HACKLE

OTHER TYPES OF WET FLIES

WOOLY WORM

GAUZE WING

KEEL FLY

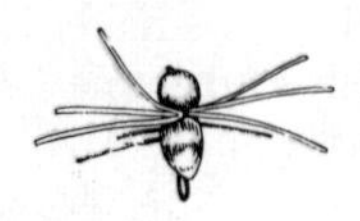
SPIDER

BASS FLY

PANFISH TEASER

Divided-Wing Patterns

** Black Gnat
** Blue Dun
** Coachman
* Coachman, Leadwing
* Cowdung
** Ginger Quill
* Gold-Ribbed Hare's Ear

March Brown
* Montreal
* Parmacheene Belle
Rio Grande King
** Royal Coachman
Stonefly
Western Bee, or McGinty

Sizes 8, 10, 12, 14 are most common.

Featherwing Patterns

Adams
Alexandra
** Cahill, Dark
** Cahill, Light
Grizzly King

Mosquito
* Professor
Queen of Waters
* Quill Gordon

Sizes 8, 10, 12, 14 are most common.

** Most frequently mentioned
* Very frequently mentioned

Hackle Patterns

** Brown Hackle	** Gray Hackle
Brown Hackle, Yellow	* Gray Hackle, Yellow
Brown Hackle, Peacock	Gray Hackle, Peacock

Sizes 6, 8, 10, 12 are most common.

Wooly worms are a hackle fly and are used in a variety of colors, especially in the western part of the country. The following colors are often used. The color here refers to body color, the hackle may be tied of the same color or a different color.

Black Wooly Worm	Gray Wooly Worm
Brown Wooly Worm	True's (Wooly Bear) Wooly Worm
Red Wooly Worm	Orange Wooly Worm
Yellow Wooly Worm	Black and Orange Wooly Worm
Green Wooly Worm	

Sizes 4, 6, 8, 10, 12 are most common.

Hairwing Patterns

Most of the traditional patterns may be ordered in hairwing styles. Three popular ones are:

* McGinty
** Royal Coachman
* Silver Doctor

Sizes 8, 10, 12, 14 are most common.

Squirrel tail flies are hairwing. Popular ones include:

Red Squirrel Tail/Red or Yellow Body
Gray Squirrel Tail/Red, or Yellow, or Gray Body
Picket Pin (Has gray squirrel tail and peacock head/ bloody butcher, or red, or yellow body.

Sizes 6, 8, 10 are most common.

** Most frequently mentioned
* Very frequently mentioned

Gauze Wing Patterns

Dan Bailey's Nature Fly Co.: Dan Bailey's Fly Shop
Sizes: 6, 8, 10, long shank hooks
Patterns: Salmon Fly—Brown and orange body and brown veined wings
Trout Fly—Brown and yellow body and gray veined wings

Rubber Body or Legs

These flies are most often used for bluegills and other sunfish, but they will also catch trout, bass, and other panfish. Some common ones are:

Dan Bailey's Rubber Legs (Girdle Bug)
Co.: Dan Bailey
Sizes: 6, 8, 10
Patterns: black, yellow, gray, brown.

Fall's Spider
Co.: Fall's Bait Co.
Sizes: 10
Patterns: black, yellow, green.

Bream Wiggler
Co.: Fall's Bait Co.
Sizes: 8
Patterns: gray squirrel hair, either black or green body, white feelers.

Skimmer Fly
Co.: Glen Evans
Sizes: 10
Patterns: black, white, yellow, green, red, brown.

Keel Fly Patterns

These are now made in dry, streamer, and wet fly patterns. They were originated by the Keel Fly Company (now a subsidiary of McClellan Industries, Burke Flexo-Products Co.) and are designed to be weedless since the hook rides upright. The following wet flies are available:

Keel Wet Fly
Co.: Keel Fly Co.
Sizes: 12, 14, 16
Patterns: gray, white, yellow, black, olive, ginger.

Panfish Flies

Any of the traditional flies will catch panfish, but this designation refers specifically to the hackle or wing type flies designed especially for panfish. The following are popular:

Hackle Spin
Co.: Fall's Bait Co.
Sizes: 2, 4, 6, 8 (use smallest sizes for panfish)
Pattern: Black Gnat, Brown Hackle, Gray Hackle, Red Ibis, White Miller, Yellow Sally.

Marathon Red Tail Crappie Fly
Co.: Marathon Bait Co.
Sizes: 4, 6, 8
Patterns: Bee, Black Gnat, Parma Belle, Royal Coachman, White Miller, Yellow Sally.

Panfish Teaser
Co.: Glen Evans
Sizes: 6
Patterns: white-red-green, white and red, or yellow and black.

Sunfisher
Co.: Falls Bait Co.
Sizes: 8
Patterns: Bee, Black Gnat, Coachman, Red Ibis, White Miller, Yellow Sally.

Tip-Top Hackle Flies
Co.: Glen Evans
Sizes: 6, 8, 10
Material: Chenille bodies, hackle
Patterns: Black Gnat, Brown Hackle, Gray Hackle, Lord Baltimore, McGinty, Yellow Sally.

Weber Brim-Fli
Co.: Weber Tackle Co.
Sizes: 4, 6, 8, 10
Material: All hackle, feather tail

Patterns: black hackle, black/red, or white tail. Yellow hackle, red tail. White hackle, red tail. Gray hackle, red tail.

Weber PanFisher Wet Fly
Co.: Weber Tackle Co.
Sizes: 4, 6, 8, 10, 12
Patterns: Black Gnat, Brown Hackle Peacock, Col. Fuller, Erie, Gray Hackle Peacock, Ibis, Lord Baltimore, McGinty, Parma Belle, Royal Coachman, White Miller, Yellow May.

Worth PanFish Fly
Co.: Worth Fishing Tackle
Sizes: 4, 6, 8, 10
Patterns: Same choices as Weber PanFisher Wet Fly above.

Bass Spinner Flies

This term designates a traditional, old style, flat-wing fly, often used in combination with a spinner while fly fishing for bass. It was developed before the newer bass bugs and streamers were used. It is still a fine fish catcher, and is used on both smallmouth and largemouth bass. The following flies are popular:

Trojan Bass Flies
Co.: Glen Evans
Sizes: 1, 2
Patterns: 6 choices: Col. Fuller, Lord Baltimore, McGinty, Ibis, Silver Doctor, Yellow Sally.

Weber Bigvalu Bass Fly
Co.: Weber Tackle Co.
Sizes: 2, 1/0
Patterns: Same 12 patterns as Weber PanFisher Wet Fly.

Weber Kleerwill Bass Fly
Co.: Weber Tackle Co.
Sizes: 2, 1/0
Patterns: Same as above Bigvalu Bass Fly except Coachman and Professor are included instead of Erie and McGinty.

There are dozens of local fly tiers across the country, but the following large companies all tie fine wet flies. See Appendix for addresses.

Dan Bailey's Fly Shop
Falls Bait Co. (Panfish hackle flies and rubber body and leg flies only)
Glen L. Evans
Hank Roberts Outfitters
Keel Fly Co. (Keel Flies only)
Marathon Bait Co. (Panfish flies only)
M. Behrens
The Orvis Co.
Phillips Fly and Tackle Co. (Wooly Worms only)
Weber Tackle Co.
Worth Fishing Tackle

NYMPHS

Nymphs are the immature larvae forms of insects which are subaqueous (live part of their life under water). Biologically speaking, the larva does not become a nymph until the rudimentary wings of the immature insect become visible. However, anglers apply the term to all of the subaqueous stages of growth of insects. Artificial nymphs are used to represent these natural larvae. The most important naturals to imitate are the mayfly nymphs, caddis larvae, and stonefly nymphs, and less importantly the dobson fly nymphs (hellgrammites), dragonfly nymphs, damselfly nymphs, cranefly larvae, midges, and others. Since there are hundred of species of some of these insects, dozens of imitations have been created to reproduce them, making the selection of artificial nymphs difficult. Also, the patterns of nymphs have not become as standardized as have those of the adult insects.

However, the following are all commonly used and ought to enable you to meet most conditions across the country. The names of some of the tackle companies where they are tied are given for each pattern to enable the buyer to obtain them if desired. Many patterns may be obtained in weighted or unweighted versions.

Recommended Patterns

** Black & Orange
** Black & Yellow
Black Midge
* Breadcrust
Brown Drake
** Caddis Fly Nymph
Damsel Fly Nymph
Dark Olive
Dragon Fly Nymph
Ed Burke Nymph
* Ginger Quill
** Gray Nymph
** Green Caddis
Hare's Ear
Hellgrammite
* Hendrickson, Dark
* March Brown
** Mayfly Nymph
Montana
* Shrimp
** Stonefly Nymph
** Tellico
Trueblood's Otter Nymph
Zug Bug

** Most frequently mentioned
* Very frequently mentioned

TYPES OF NYMPHS

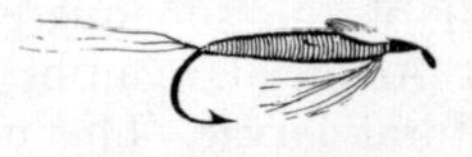
DARK HENDRICKSON

STONEFLY CREEPER

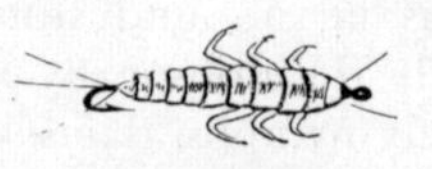
MAYFLY NYMPH

STONEFLY NYMPH

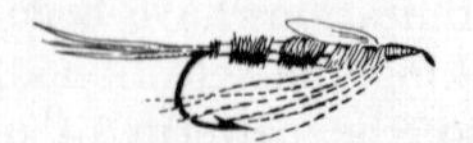
MARCH BROWN

The following companies offer a wide variety of nymphs. See Appendix for addresses.

Dan Bailey's Fly Shop
Glen L. Evans
Hank Roberts Outfitters
M. Behrens
The Orvis Co.
Phillips Fly and Tackle Co.
Weber Tackle Co.
Worth Fishing Tackle

STREAMER FLIES

Streamer flies are generally divided into three basic types according to the material of which they are made: *hair, feather,* and *maribou.* In addition to these three, *streamer keel flies* might be mentioned. They may be tied of the same materials as any one of the three other types, but with a special keel-type hood designed to ride upright.

Hair streamers are usually made of deer hair or bucktail; polar bear hair is used for some patterns. They are the most durable of the three types of streamers. They do lack the advantage of natural multicolor markings which can be obtained in feathers, but they are dyed different colors to obtain the desired effect.

Feather streamers utilize hackle and other feathers, of a variety of colors to give the effect of minnows or other small fish. The limber feathers create a "breathing" (in and out) movement when the fly is retrieved in jerks, a motion which is very attractive to fish.

Maribou streamers are made of maribou feathers in various colors. These streamers are attractor-type flies that depend upon their quivering wing action to tempt strikes. Maribou streamers are the least durable of the three types of streamers, but they are highly effective fish catchers for a variety of gamefish.

As with other types of flies, the author has consulted experts all over the U.S. to get their recommendations of favorite patterns for different fish. The list of streamer flies below do not include all patterns, but they do include some of the best ones. Specific recommendations for each species of fish are given in later sections of this book. Streamer patterns which are used primarily for steelhead or Atlantic salmon are discussed in a separate chapter. The patterns listed are all fine trout streamers, but many of them are used even more extensively for landlocked salmon, bass, or panfish, with some even used for pike and pickerel.

Feather Streamer Patterns

Barnes Special
Black Demon, Cain's River
** Black Ghost
Chappie
Golden Darter
Golden Witch
** Gray Ghost
* Green Ghost
Grizzly King
Jane Craig
Lady Ghost
Montreal
Nine-Three
* Parmacheene Belle
Parson Tom
Professor
Roaring Rapids
* Royal Coachman
Spruce Fly
** Supervisor
Yellow Perch

Sizes 2, 4, 6, 8, 10, 12 are all used, depending on the fish taken and the water fished.

** Most frequently mentioned
* Very frequently mentioned

BASIC TYPES OF STREAMERS

BUCKTAIL

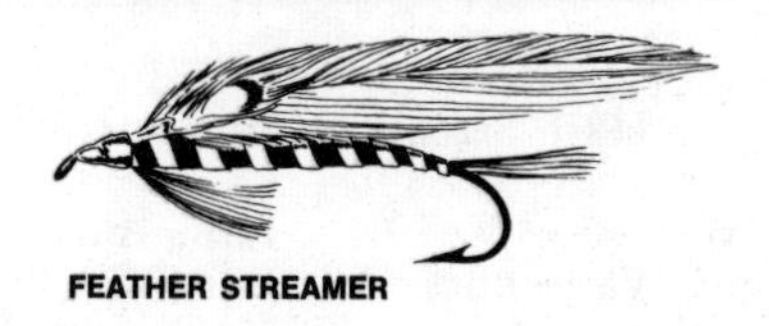

FEATHER STREAMER

MARIBOU

In addition to these "New England" feather streamer flies just listed, manufacturers have developed several specialized feather streamers for a variety of uses.

Mylar feather streamers, like the mylar hair streamers, have an addition of Dupont mylar along each side to give added flash.

Multi-wing feather streamers have a bushy hackle collar and several widely forked hackle streamer tails which wave vigorously during the retrieve. These flies are usually used in large sizes, sometimes with a spinner attached, for bass, large trout, salmon, pike, pickerel, muskies, or saltwater fish.

Marathon Crappie Minnow and *Evan's Crappie-Bluegill Flies* are original creations developed primarily for panfish.

The *Optic* and *Erskine Shiner Minnow* are feathered streamers with enlarged eyes to represent the tiny fry of fish.

Hair Streamer Patterns

Alaska Mary Ann
* Black and White Bucktail
** Black Nosed Dace
Blonde Bucktails (See separate discussion which follows)
Brown and White Bucktail
Brown and Yellow Bucktail
Brown Squirrel, Yellow
** Edson Tiger, Dark
** Edson Tiger, Light
Gov. Aiken
Green Cosseboom
Gray Squirrel, Red
Little Brook Trout
Little Brown Trout
Little Rainbow Trout
Magog Smelt
** Mickey Finn
** Muddler Minnow (See separate discussion which follows)
* Royal Coachman Bucktail
Red and Black Bucktail
* Red and White Bucktail
Red Squirrel Tail
Worden's Worry
White Bucktail
Yellow and Black Bucktail
Yellow Bucktail

Sizes 2, 4, 6, 8, 10, 12 are all used, depending on the type and size of fish.

** Most frequently mentioned
* Very frequently mentioned

Blonde bucktails are tied in large sizes (#2–4/0) because they were originally developed for saltwater use. However, they are becoming increasingly popular for freshwater use, especially for Coho salmon, bass, pike, and even large trout (especially out West in sizes #2–1/0).

The *Muddler Minnow* is probably the most important trout streamer fly used in the streams of the Western United States. It is a versatile fly, since it can be fished dry, or wet, slow, or skipped over the surface, cast or trolled. It is now made in other patterns in addition to the natural bucktail.

Dan Bailey's Fly Shop sells a special bucktail streamer fly with mylar added to the body. It is called a *Mylar Body Bucktail Streamer*. Mylar is a plastic metallic substance often tied along the sides of streamers to give added flash. Now it comes as mylar tubing so is used for the fly body in these flies by Dan Bailey. Orvis also sells regular mylar streamers.

Maribou Streamer Patterns

** Black Maribou
Black and Yellow Maribou
* White Maribou
Yellow Maribou

** Most frequently mentioned
* Very frequently mentioned

Maribou is also used in combination with other types of materials to make some unique fish-getting streamers.

Maribou muddlers utilize maribou feathers in muddler minnow styles resulting in increasingly popular flies in a variety of patterns.

Mylar maribou streamer flies combine the flash of mylar with the wavy action of the maribou feathers.

There are many tiers across the country that tie and sell excellent streamer flies, but the list of companies below represents some of the large fly tiers. See Appendix for addresses.

Dan Bailey's Fly Shop
Glen L. Evans
Hank Roberts Outfitters
Keel Fly Co. (keel flies only)
Marathon Bait Co. (Marathon Minnow only)
M. Behrens
The Orvis Co.
Phillips Fly and Tackle Co.
Weber Tackle Co.
Worth Fishing Tackle

TERRESTRIALS

The term terrestrial as it applies to fishing flies is a fairly new one. It refers to a whole group of artificials which imitate land insects which may fall, crawl, or jump in the water and provide food for fish. According to this definition, any imitation of a land bug, beetle, roach, cricket, hopper, or fly is a terrestrial. There are thousands of species of these in nature; artificials to represent them could go on without limit. Actually, there are only a few basic groups which have been developed.

Ants represent flying ants.
Beetles represent a whole group of natural beetles.
Crickets represent their counterpart in nature.
Grasshoppers, hopper flies, Hornberg flies all represent grasshoppers.
Inch worms represent their counterpart in nature.
Jassids are very small imitations which represent a variety of natural land insects.

TYPES OF TERRESTRIALS

ANT

BEETLE

GRASSHOPPER

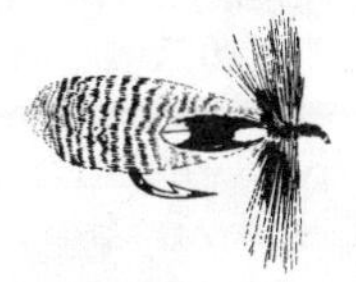

HORNBERG

INCH WORM

JASSID

Ant Patterns

** Black
Brown
Cinnamon
Natural
* Red
* Red and Black
White
Wood Ant
Yellow and Black

Beetle Patterns

* Black
Bronze
Brown
Green

Jassids

** Black body, black hackle
Orange body, brown hackle
Yellow body, ginger hackle

** Most frequently mentioned
* Very frequently mentioned

SALMON AND STEELHEAD FLIES

Salmon Flies

The term salmon flies is generally used with one salmon in mind: the Atlantic salmon. Flies for this fish have been wet flies, traditionally, tied on heavy, strong hooks in sizes from #10 up to as large as #6/0. Since the Atlantic salmon does not feed after it enters the spawning river, the fly patterns do not have to represent natural insects. Rather, the patterns are designed to attract the fish and tease it into striking; therefore they are usually gay and gaudy, especially those used in the high water of early season. As the summer turns into fall, patterns become more somber and sizes smaller, and the dry fly comes into its own. As a matter of fact, dry flies are used more and more in the rivers of Maine and New Brunswick throughout the summer, after the water warms up to about 60 degrees. Also, fishermen are discovering the usefulness of many traditional trout patterns—for example, the Wulff dry flies, Irresistible, and the Muddler Minnow. Also, even the traditional New England feather streamers—Gray Ghost, Black Ghost, and Edson Tiger Dark—will catch fish (especially early in the season near the mouth of the river) even though Atlantics are not supposed to take streamer flies. Specific recommendations of all types are given in the section on Atlantic Salmon. The purpose here is only to list the most important salmon fly patterns. The concluding portion of this section offers a word about flies for Pacific salmon and Landlocked salmon.

Atlantic Salmon Patterns

The list below does not include all patterns, nor even all of the good ones, but it does contain many of the best ones, all of which are proven fish getters and which will provide a wide assortment for the angler. The flies should all be tied wet, unless otherwise designated. The list does not include many traditional trout fly patterns, even those which are often used for Atlantic salmon, since these patterns are discussed in the sections on dry flies and wet flies. Also, see the section on Atlantic salmon for complete recommendations of all flies.

Amherst
Black Bear Hair
Black Doctor
** Black Dose
Black Rat
* Blue Charm
Brown Bomber
Cinnamon Sedge (Dry)
* Conrad
Cosseboom
Deadly McIntosh (Dry)
* Durham Ranger
** Dusty Miller
Fiery Brown
* Green Highlander
** Jock Scott
Lady Amherst
Mar Lodge
Nepisquit Gray
Night Hawk
Red Abbey
Silver Blue
** Silver Doctor
** Silver Gray
* Silver Rat
Silver Wilkerson
** Thunder and Lightning

** Most frequently mentioned
* Very frequently mentioned

Pacific Salmon Flies

Few flies have been developed specifically for the different species of Pacific salmon, since only a few of these salmon are caught on flies. Those flies which have been developed have been primarily the saltwater bucktail streamers and the large feather, multi-wing patterns. These flies have been used primarily for coho salmon and to a lesser extent for king salmon. (Some king or chinook salmon are caught upstream on standard trout-fly patterns in large sizes.) Occasionally, humpback or pink salmon and kokanee salmon (landlocked sockeyes) are caught on flies. Sockeye salmon and chum or dog salmon are not taken readily by anglers anyhow.

Increasingly, however, fishermen are experimenting with New England type streamers and traditional trout flies for coho salmon. Since cohos have been introduced into the Great Lakes and other large, inland waters, more and more flies and lures are and will be developed specifically for them. See the section on Pacific Salmon for additional information.

Landlocked Salmon Flies

To the easterner, landlocked salmon means landlocked Atlantic salmon. To the resident of the Pacific Northwest, it means landlocked sockeye or kokanee salmon. No special flies have been developed for kokanee, since they are more often caught by snagging than by fishing with flies, lures, or bait. Most of the New England type of streamer flies were developed primarily for landlocked Atlantic salmon as well as for trout. See the sections on Streamer Flies and on Kokanee, Landlocked and Ouananiche Salmon for specific recommendations.

Steelhead Flies

Steelhead are sea-run rainbow trout which return to the rivers to spawn. They are one of the most popular fish in the Pacific Northwest, and, since they take flies readily, a number of patterns have been developed especially for them. It is these flies which are listed here. The best steelhead flies are tied wet, and are sparsely dressed so they will sink readily. A number of Atlantic salmon patterns and trout patterns are also used for steelhead. For complete recommendations of flies and lures see the section on Steelhead.

Al's Special
* Babine Special
* Boss
Brad's Brat
* Burlap
Carson
* Cole's Comet
Copper Demon
* Cummings Special
* Doctor Rex
* Fall Favorite
* Golden Demon
Gorden's Favorite
Hargee's Sea Shrimp
Horners Silver Shrimp
* Hoyt's Killer
Humboldt Railbird
Improved Governor
* Jock Scott
Joe O'Donnell
Juicy Bug
** Kalema Special
Lady Godiva
* Marietta
* McLeod Ugly
Nite Hawk
* Orange Demon
Orange Optic
Orange Shrimp
* Polar Shrimp
Princess
Purple Peril
Queen Bess
Railbird
* Rogue Special
* Royal Coachman
Sally
Sammy Fly
Silver Admiral
Silver Demon
* Silver Doctor
** Silver Hilton
Silver Wilkerson
Siwash Special
** Skunk
** Skykomish Sunrise
Spitfire
* Thor
Umpqua Red Brat
** Umpqua Special
Van Luren
Weatherwax
* Yellow Hammer

** Most frequently mentioned
* Very frequently mentioned

PART III

Baits

BAITFISH

Alewife

The alewife is one of four fish of the Herring family (the other three are sardine, shad, menhaden) found in the ocean from Labrador to Florida, and landlocked in the St. Lawrence River drainage, the Mississippi valley, and the Great Lakes. In salt water it grows to over a foot, but in fresh water it is usually only 3 to 6 inches. It ascends rivers and streams to spawn, whether from the ocean or lakes. It is useful as a baitfish in those waters already containing it. Bass like it, and it is even used some as a baitfish for trout in states where it is found naturally. It can be kept best in non-crowded conditions in a bait well in the center of the boat, or in a wash tube with a cake of ice.

Eels

The freshwater eel known as a mud eel is really the American brook lamprey and is a harmless member of the family to which the parasitic sea lamprey belongs. Like other lampreys, it spends part of life buried in the mud of a brook or stream where it can be dug up with a hay fork. These immature eels are about 6 or 7 inches long, and are found principally in streams of Ohio, Kentucky, West Virginia, and other midwestern states. Actually, they exist everywhere except the Rocky Mountain area and the Deep South. They are tough, long-lasting baits, and are a favorite of bass. They can also be used for walleyes, pike, and pickerel.

Minnows

Minnow is a general term used to designate any small fish which is used for bait. To be more precise, however, a minnow is any fish belonging to the family Cyprinidae, which includes the carp and goldfish as well as the smaller minnows. All of these fish are spring or summer spawners. Only a few species are vegetarians; the others eat both animal and vegetable substances. Carp root up vegetation from the bottom and keep the water continually discolored; this habit, along with their destruction of the spawn of other fish, makes them a highly undesirable species. The angler must be extremely careful, therefore, never to use carp minnows as bait or to introduce carp into any waters.

There are nearly 2,000 species of fish in the minnow family, of which 192 are found in the United States. The most common minnows in this country are *shiners, chubs, daces,* and just *"minnows."*

In general, shiners are the least hardy; they are harder to keep alive and they die sooner on the hook than any others. The chubs are the most hardy and stay lively on the hook for longer periods of time. The daces and common minnows rank somewhere in between.

Shad

The two most important species of shad which are stocked in freshwater as forage fish and which are used as baitfish are the gizzard shad (*Dorosoma cepedianum*) and the threadfin shad (*Dorosoma petenense*). The gizzard shad grows larger (to over 12 inches) so does not afford food for as long as does the threadfin shad (which usually grows to only 6 to 8 inches). Both have been stocked in reservoirs as forage fish, where the largemouth bass and white bass feed heavily upon them. They make excellent bait for bass, white bass especially, but are hard to keep alive. One trick is to use a large bait well in the boat, or to put a cake of ice in the center of a tub. The shad swim around the tub without hitting their heads against the sides. Dead shad can be used as a bait for catfish.

Smelt

The most important smelt, the American smelt (*Osmerus mordax*), is a cold-water fish which lives in the ocean, but which is found landlocked in the Great Lakes and in many lakes of the northeastern United States. It is one of the most important baitfish in New England, used primarily for landlocked salmon and trout, both during the summer and through the ice in the winter. It is also caught in the larger sizes as a fine food fish in its own right.

Another smelt, the pond smelt (*Hipomesus olidus*), is found primarily in freshwater in Alaska and northwestern Canada.

Suckers

The term *sucker* is the name given to a number of kinds of fish closely related to the minnow family. They have small mouths on the underneath side of the jaw, with thick, fleshy lips that enable them to suck up food. The sucker family is extremely large, but two of the most common species are: the white sucker (*Catostomus commersonii*), the commonest of all the suckers, found throughout the United States; and the northern redhorse sucker (*Maxostoma macrolepidotum*), one of the most colorful suckers, found in the North and Central states east of the Rockies, south to Kansas and Arkansas and east to New York and Pennsylvania.

Because of their fairly large size, suckers are used extensively as bait for the larger freshwater fish—pike and muskies especially. Smaller ones are used as bait for bass, pickerel, and other fish.

EARTHWORMS, NIGHTCRAWLERS

There are more than 2,000 species of earthworms found in the world but most of them are never used as bait. In the United States, the three species most commonly used are the common night crawler (*Lumbricus terrestris*), the manure worm (*Eisenia foetida*), and the ordinary earthworm (*Helodrilus caliginosus*).

Earthworms are probably the most universal of all fish baits. They are used for most species of freshwater fish: trout, some salmon, bass, walleyes, and the various species of panfish. They are not often used for pike and muskies, nor for some salmon. Nevertheless, they are used by fishermen in every state of the union.

Obtaining Worms

By far the best way of obtaining earthworms, as far as I am concerned, is to buy them in quantity lots from wholesale bait dealers. Most local dealers that sell them by the dozen charge far more than do the wholesale dealers. All of the outdoor magazines run ads offering worms for sale. Prices usually range from $4 to $7 per 1,000, with most dealers charging between $4 and $5.

If you do want to gather your own earthworms, however, there are several methods. When the worms are near the surface (as they will be during periods of wet, mild weather), they can be easily obtained by using any one of a number of electric-shock devices. Or a metal stake can be driven into the ground and then pounded with a hammer to produce vibrations in the soil which send the worms in the surrounding area scurrying to the surface. Various chemical solutions can also be obtained to pour over the ground to chase worms from their burrows. You can make your own solution by dissolving one bichloride of mercury tablet per gallon of water or by mixing a strong solution of mustard and water. When such chemicals are used, the worms ought to be washed thoroughly after being captured. Please remember, however, that these methods are only appropriate when the worms are thickly distributed and near the surface of the ground. During very hot, cold, or dry weather, these methods are fruitless.

The time-honored method of obtaining worms is by digging them with a spading fork. Try to select damp areas of rich soil such as along creeks or rivers, near drain-offs of septic tanks, in barnyards, or in moist, shaded areas in meadows. In dry weather, you can make your job easier by watering a wormy section of land for several days before spading.

The easiest and most common way of gathering night crawlers is by searching for them on most lawns after dark. If the evening is moderately cool, and the soil and lawn moist, the night crawlers will come to the surface and crawl out of their holes after dark. You must be careful in shining your light that the very bright beam does not hit the crawlers directly or they will retreat into their holes. Some people use a red beam, which does not frighten the worms. Care must also be taken in packing up the crawlers so that they will not be broken as they are pulled from their holes.

Manure worms can be found in any type of manure in barns and farmyards. These worms can even be gathered in winter since the manure usually does not freeze.

Keeping Worms

Worms that are to be kept for short periods of time may be placed in a cool place in sphagnum moss, leaves, Buss-bedding, or peat moss with a small amount of feed. Before being used, worms ought to be placed in your bait container with sphagnum moss (the kind obtained from a florist) to be scoured. This means the worms get rid of the earth inside of them while in the moss and become more transparent, and, at the same time, tougher and more lively.

It is important to keep worms damp since they obtain their oxygen from the water in the soil. It is all right to put a lid on the container, even one that shuts out all air. In fact, a tight lid is needed on any nightcrawler container to keep the worms from escaping.

LAND INSECTS AND THEIR LARVAE

Included under this heading are a variety of land-dwelling (terrestrial) insects, many completely different and unrelated, but all commonly used as bait, especially for panfish.

Catalpa Worms

This worm has been crowned by many fishermen, especially those of the Midwest and South, as the finest bluegill bait obtainable. The worm is the

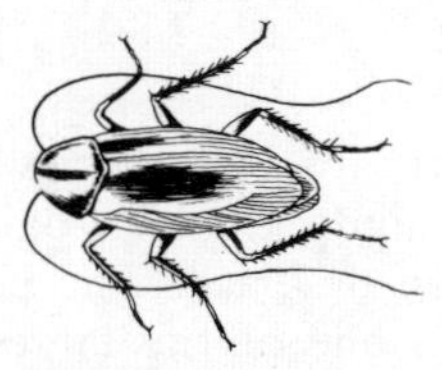

SPHINX MOTH LARVA   COCKROACH

larva of the sphinx moth which lays its eggs on catalpa trees (these can be identified by their broad leaves and bean pods). After the larvae hatch, they feed on the leaves of the tree until about 3 inches long and too fat to hold on; they then drop to the ground where they burrow in, form pupae and eventually hatch into moths. The worms are dark brown in color, or black, with green along the sides. They are smooth-skinned and very tough baits. You can often catch a half-dozen or more fish with one worm.

Some fishermen prefer to turn the worm inside out with a stick or nail, either using a half or all of the worm as bait. The worms can be kept for long periods of time if fed catalpa leaves. Or they can be placed in corn meal and put in your refrigerator and kept dormant for a few weeks until used.

Cockroaches

There are four common species of cockroaches: German, Oriental, American, and Wood. The German or Croton bug (*Blattella germanica*) and American cockroach (*Periplaneta americana*) are most common and are easiest to raise. They can be found in barns, garbage dumps, wharehouses, and other places. The can be caught easiest in insect traps with raw or cooked vegetables, apples, or moist bread as bait. They prefer dark places and usually come out of hiding at night.

Crickets

There are two species of field crickets which are commonly used as bait: the gray and the dark-brown or black. The latter species (*Gryllus assimilis*) is one of the largest and is usually preferred.

Crickets can be most easily found late in the summer and in the fall under stones, hay piles, and in wheat, corn, or rye stacks. They can be baited and gathered by scattering stale bread to lure them. Or take sheafs of oats or wheat and shake the crickets into a barrel or tub. They can be kept in the same type of containers used for grasshoppers and fed grass, lettuce, or chicken mash. If crickets are kept for very long, they can be supplied with water in shallow dishes which have been filled with cotton to keep the crickets from drowning.

Gall Worms

This is the common name given to a variety of larvae of flies and wasps which grow inside the stems of various plants. Each insect selects a specific plant. The adults lay their eggs in the plant tissue. As the eggs hatch, the tissue swells and forms a hardened gall completely surrounding the larvae. The larvae form pupae inside the gall and the adult emerges by burrowing through the side.

The most common galls are found on oak apples, on blackberry bushes, and on goldenrod. Galls can be collected in the fall or early winter, kept in a cool, dry place until needed and then split open when bait is required. The larvae make excellent bait for bluegills and trout.

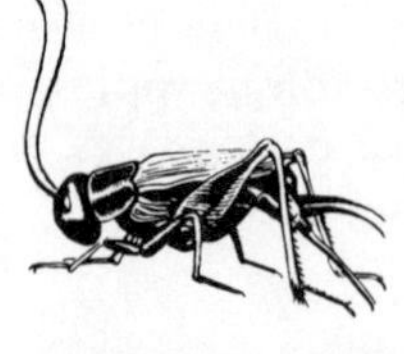

CRICKET

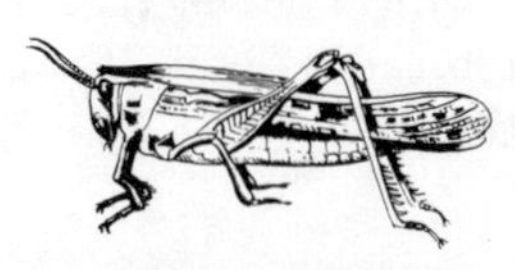

AMERICAN GRASSHOPPER

Grasshoppers

There are many species; some seem better than others. The large, gray-brown, flying grasshoppers are too hard to catch and are too large for many small panfish and trout; others, like the very small, light-green ones, are too delicate to use as bait. Since grasshoppers are found throughout the United States, however, there will usually be more than enough of the right species in any locale to use for bait. They are especially numerous during the hot weather of late summer and early fall and are most effective to use then.

The big problem is to catch them. A small butterfly net or large fly swatter will help you to pin them to the ground to grab them. The best way to get them, however, is to collect them in the early morning when the grass is wet with dew and the air is cool; under these conditions, the insects can scarcely fly or jump at all.

Grasshoppers can be kept in any light, cheesecloth bag or insect box with a fine-mesh screen. Ordinary grass leaves make good food for them. The insects should be kept dry and warm. Some fishermen use a small, light wooden box with screen wire over the ends to keep grasshoppers in. Put a piece of old innertube over a large hole in the top with a 2-inch slit. The fisherman can reach down through the hole to get some bait without other insects escaping.

If you want to use grasshoppers for bait year-round, gather them in season and put them in your freezer until needed. They make excellent bait for ice fishing for bluegills and perch.

Grubs

There are over 100 American species of grubs, which are the larvae form of June bugs or May

MAY BEETLE

MEAL WORM LARVA

beetles. The beetles lay their white eggs in the ground, where they hatch and where the white grubs feed for two or three years. They pupate underground in the fall and adults appear the following spring. The adults feed on the leaves of many common trees. One species, commonly called the green June beetle, is most common in the South and Southeast where they do considerable damage to apricots, grapes, melons, and other fruits. The grubs are delicate and need to be tied on a hook or impaled through the head. They can be kept in the same type of earth as that in which they are found.

Maggots

Although many people are repelled at the thought of using maggots, these larvae make excellent baits. The most common are maggots from the housefly, the black horsefly or stable fly, the greenbottle and bluebottle flies, and the blowfly.

Blowfly larvae can be obtained by hanging a piece of meat or a small animal outdoors in warm weather. The blowflies lay their eggs on the meat; the larvae hatch out and, in about a week, mature, fattening maggots are available for bait. Place the maggots in corn meal where they will dry out, be scoured and become more pleasant to use for bait.

Meal Worms

These are another popular bait, especially in the winter for ice fishing. They are the larvae of darkling beetles and mealworm beetles. A common species is the *Tenebrio obscurus,* which is known as the dark meal worm. Another species, the *Tenebrio molitor,* is known as the yellow meal worm. Both are excellent baits. These larvae can be found wherever grain is stored; in grainaries, feed stores, pet shops, poultry houses, and other places. The beetles lay their eggs in the grain, hatch out as larvae, and eventually grow into other beetles.

WATER INSECTS, THEIR NYMPHS OR LARVAE

Water insects and their nymphs or larvae are eaten at one time or another by most fish. For this reason, they make excellent bait if they are the right size.

In the process of development from egg to adult, the insect goes through a series of stages. Some go through three stages: egg, nymph, adult; others develop in four: egg, larva, pupa, and adult. The most commonly used baits are described below:

Caddis Worms

These are the larvae of the caddis fly, which lays hundreds of eggs on submerged rocks or plants while flying over the water. After hatching, the larvae build portable, protective cases or sacks of sticks, leaves, stones, sand, and other materials, cemented together with a special secretion. The larva lives in this case, dragging it around wherever it goes. Look for them moving around in the quieter waters of streams or shorelines of lakes where they can be seined or picked up by hand. The worm itself should be removed from the case before it is threaded on the fish hook.

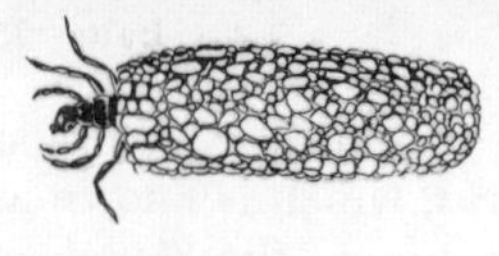

CADDIS FLY

CRANE-FLY LARVA

Since there are over 200 species of these insects, ordinarily only those which produce the largest larvae can be used for bait. The larvae can be kept in tanks of cool water, although they are cannibalistic in captivity.

Crane-Fly Larvae

The adult crane fly is a "daddy-longlegs" sort of insect, sometimes mistaken for a large mosquito. There are about 300 species in the United States; the larvae of some live in water, but most live on land in damp, decomposing earth. Those living in water can be obtained by shoveling or raking up material from the stream or lake bottom and washing over a wire screen. The larvae can be gathered off the screen. Commercial bait dealers handle a larva known as *mousee*. This is a species of crane-fly larva; it is excellent bait for ice fishing for bluegills.

Dragonfly Nymphs

These are often called perch bugs in many parts of the country. They live in ponds, lakes, and the quieter sections of streams where they hide in the mud and vegetation. They live from one to more than three years in the water, then crawl onto a stem of a water plant, a branch or a stump, where the skin of the larvae splits, allowing the adult to emerge.

These nymphs can be obtained by dragging a seine with a weighted bottom edge over the muddy bottom of stream or lake or through water plants.

Or you can rake or shovel up the bottom muck and debris, carefully looking for these nymphs. Once obtained, they can be kept in tanks of water. They will live for short periods of time in your bait container to which moistened moss has been added.

Damselfly Nymphs

These are more delicate than the dragonfly nymphs, having longer, thinner bodies and legs. They are obtained and kept alive in the same way as dragonfly nymphs. They should not be stored with dragonfly nymphs, however, as both are cannibalistic.

Hellgrammites

These are the larval form of the big, winged insect known as the Dobson fly. The fly lays several thousand eggs on branches, rocks, or other objects along a stream. After hatching, the tiny larvae drop into the water where they grow and develop (as hellgrammites) for nearly three years. At two years and eleven months the mature hellgrammite emerges, hides under a log or stone for about a month, and changes into the adult Dobson fly.

Hellgrammites are most numerous in fast-water streams. They can be gathered by holding a wire screen or seine across a portion of the stream and turning over rocks immediately upstream of the screen so that the larvae wash into it. A rake or hoe is a helpful tool to use in overturning the rocks.

DRAGONFLY NYMPH

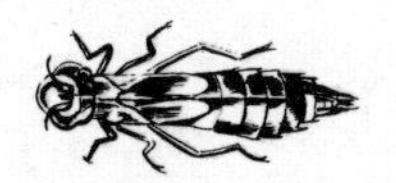

DAMSELFLY NYMPH

Hellgrammites range in size from about 1 to 3 inches; the smaller ones are better for panfish or trout, the larger for smallmouth bass. Hellgrammites can be kept for a long time in running water, or they will live for weeks in a cool cellar. Put them in a box along with dampened leaves or moss. Keep them damp but not too wet. They can be transferred to your bait box to which some damp moss has been added at the time you go fishing. Feed the larvae small amounts of ground beef to prevent cannibalism. Before you fish with a hellgrammite, break off the pincers on the end of the tail to keep it from clinging to stones or sticks in the water.

Mayfly Nymphs

These nymphs are the nymphal, or second stage of development of the familiar mayfly. There are many species, the nymphs varying greatly in size and shape. One of the largest is the nymph of the burrowing mayfly. The nymph may reach close to 2 inches in length. They live in mud in water depths of from a few inches to 40 feet. They can be scooped up with the mud in areas where they are plentiful and separated by washing the mud over a wire screen.

Other species of these nymphs prefer clear, rocky streams where they cling to stones in the riffles and from where they can be seined. Others swim around in the shallows of lakes or streams.

All species can be kept in tanks of cool, well-aerated water. The bottoms of tanks should be

HELLGRAMMITE

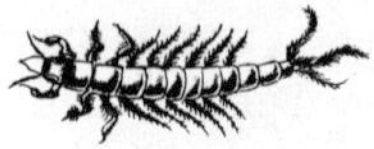

MAYFLY NYMPH

covered with material similar to the stream or lake bottoms where found. Place the nymphs in a bait container filled with damp, cool moss. They can be kept in a minnow bucket of cold water for short periods of time.

Stonefly Nymphs

These nymphs are sometimes mistaken for mayfly nymphs, although the two are unrelated. However, stonefly nymphs prefer fast-running streams where they cling to the underside of stones. They can be

STONEFLY NYMPH

caught by placing a wire screen across streams, then lifting up stones upstream of the screen so that the nymphs may be washed into it.

CRUSTACEANS

Clams, Mussels

Freshwater clams or mussels are readily obtainable in the lakes and streams of the northern section of the United States, and make excellent bait for bluegills, other sunfish, yellow perch, and bullheads. Clams may be kept alive in a box partly submerged in the lake or stream, or, for short periods of time, in containers filled with water. Crush the shells with a hammer, or open them with a knife. Use the clams raw, but cut off bite-size pieces.

Clams for use as catfish stink bait may be cured in sour milk. Cut the clams in pieces, let them soak in the milk solution in the hot sun. When it begins to smell it's ready to use.

Crawfish

This crustacean is a favorite of many bass fishermen, especially smallmouth fishermen. In smaller sizes, it can also be used as an excellent panfish bait, especially for yellow perch, bullheads, and rock bass. Crawfish are also excellent bait for trout.

There are many species; some are found in swamps, small ponds and lakes; others live in fast-moving streams. If you want to collect your own, the best way is to seine them at night, since they come out of hiding then. Seine around shallow-water weed beds or in rocky areas. Have two people handle the seine and a third follow along, pointing the flashlight at the center of the net. After the crawfish are disturbed, they will travel toward the light. Another way to catch them is with a dip net and flashlight. Other fishermen prefer to use wire traps with funnel entrances,, baiting the trap with dead fish or meat. Most of those caught in traps will be hardshells.

All crawfish grow by moulting or shedding their skin. Right after the shell is cast off the crawfish is known as "softshell." When the new shell starts to harden a day or so later, it is called a "papershell." When this shell hardens, it is called a "hardshell."

Most fishermen prefer softshells and so try to devise all sorts of ways to soften the shells. The best way, however, is to force-fatten the crawfish. Place them in a metal tank, or a screen-covered live box. The chief requirement is to have fresh, well-aerated water. A wooden box with a screen at each end, placed in a stream, is good. A tank into which air is pumped will work; or use one large enough to keep the crawfish fresh without the need for pumped air or running water. Feed them a diet of meat, dead fish, or corn meal. They will grow fast before the shells begin to peel. You can prevent the shells from hardening rapidly by putting the crawfish in moss and storing them for several days in your refrigerator. Try to keep the softshelled crawfish, and the smaller ones, separated from the hardshells and larger ones so that the latter won't kill the others.

Shrimp

There are numerous species of both freshwater and saltwater shrimp which are used as fish bait. Large saltwater shrimp may be purchased fresh (if you live along the coast) or frozen, and cut into bite-size pieces for fishing for bluegills, other sunfish, yellow perch, and bullheads. Small saltwater shrimp about an inch to an inch and a half long may be caught along bays, inlets, and tidal creeks with a long-handled net or a fine mesh seine. Brackish-water bass along the coast love all varieties of live shrimp.

A small, translucent freshwater species, sometimes called fairy shrimp, may be obtained along rushes and weedbeds in some streams or lakes. They make excellent bait for trout or panfish.

Snails, Slugs

Snails are an important part of the diet of some species of sunfishes (shellcrackers for example), but they must be removed from the shell before using. They make excellent bait for sunfish, and, to a lesser extent, for yellow perch and bullheads, Slugs are not really crustacea, since they do not have hard outer shells (they are shell-less land snails), but they may be used as bait for bass, panfish, and trout. They can be found under stones, logs, or on rotting boards or other damp places.

AMPHIBIANS, MISCELLANEOUS

Frogs, Tadpoles

If the small ones are used, frogs make excellent bait for bass, pike, pickerel, walleyes, yellow perch, and bullheads. The green frog (*Rana clamitans*), leopard frog (*Rana pipiens*), pickerel frog (*Rana palustris*) or other small species can be used.

Frogs can be found and caught along muddy, marshy ponds, streams, and rivers. Small farm ponds provide a constant source of supply in some areas. Grassy fields and meadows adjacent to water often contain thousands of frogs. They can be caught easily at night with the aid of a flashlight. A small-meshed net helps in the daytime.

Frogs can be kept alive for a long time in a live box placed in the shallow water of a lake or stream. Place rocks in it on which the frogs can rest, or put them in a well-ventilated container with damp moss or leaves. If kept reasonably cool, these frogs will live several weeks, even without food. They can be fed worms or insects that are alive and moving. A small wooden box with screen and hinged cover (or with the lid covered by an innertube) is the preferred bait box.

Tadpoles are sometimes used for bait, but since they are soft and delicate, and not nearly as hardy as frogs, they are not used as often.

Leeches

Leeches or bloodsuckers vary in size from less than an inch to 4 or more inches long when stretched out. They have sucking discs at each end of the body and live by sucking blood from various animals. They can be caught in traps baited with blood or meat. Some fishermen rub their waders with liver or bloody meat, wade through a pool where leeches are found, and then remove them from the outside of the waders. They are not often used as bait, but are very durable on a hook, and excellent for bass, yellow perch, bullheads, or trout.

Salamanders

Salamanders, waterdogs, or mudpuppies, as they are sometimes called, are one of the most used and effective baits for bass in some parts of the country. They are also effective for pike, pickerel, and walleyes even though they are not very often used for these species.

The salamander is an amphibian, and can live in streams and ponds, or on the land beneath stones, or in caves or rotten logs where it is cool, dark, and moist. They eat grubs, slugs, worms, and insects. There are many species, most of which are small. The spotted salamander of North America, one of the best-known species, is approximately 6 inches long and has yellow spots on its smooth, dark-colored skin. The red salamander, another common variety, also grows to be about 6 inches long.

PREPARED BAITS

Blood Baits

These are used primarily as catfish bait. One recipe calls for coagulated chicken blood. Let it dry in the sun for several hours and cut into balls of suitable size. Used alone it will not stay on the hook very well. You can increase its tenacity by putting strips of mosquito netting in the blood before it is hard, or cotton balls, or pieces of sponge rubber. The netting, cotton, or sponge rubber can be fastened on the hook and stands up very well.

Another recipe calls for any type of chicken or animal blood. Place the chicken or animal blood in a cloth sack which is hung up to let the plasma drip out. Then mix the blood with pieces of cotton and let harden.

There are several commercially prepared blood baits on the market, such as the Lazy Ike Bloody Bait for Catfish and the Uncle Josh Blood Bait.

Cheese Baits

Cheese is one of the most commonly used and more successful baits for trout, especially for rainbow trout, and to a lesser extent, for brook trout and brown trout. It is also a favorite bait for catfish. The cheese is sometimes cut into small portions and molded directly on the hook. At other times it is used to flavor dough or to saturate rubber or cotton. Fishermen use a variety of exotic cheese preparations, among them garlic cheese and Limburger cheese. A fairly strong, smelly cheese seems to work the best.

A good paste cheese may be made at home. Add 1 quart of boiling water to 1 pint of cornmeal and heat. Stir to keep the meal from sticking, adding small chunks of rancid cheese. Keep mixing until the mush has the consistency of rubber and will roll around the pan. Remove, place on a board sprinkled with cornmeal, and knead the dough, putting in small pieces of cotton until the dough is very tough and rubbery. Pinch off pieces and roll into small balls. You can keep the bait fresh by rolling it in a damp cloth.

There are also commercial preparations on the market. Two of the best are Uncle Josh Trout Cheese Bait and Uncle Josh Catfish Cheese Bait.

Dough Baits

These have been developed primarily for fishing for carp. When flavored with cheese, they make excellent trout bait. Or flavored as stink baits, they are used for catfish.

Each fishermen has a different recipe for making dough balls. The simplest is to use flour and water and to form into balls. Boiling the balls briefly gives them firmness so they stay on the hook better than raw dough. Mixing raw dough with cotton also adds firmness.

Another recipe is to mix half cornmeal and half flour, add water and knead. Additional strength is obtained by kneading in some cotton batting. Form into small pebbles.

Doughballs can be made into trout bait or catfish bait by adding a quantity of smelly cheese to the dough. Stink bait for catfish is made by soaking the doughballs in various aromatic solutions. An oily, fishy solution can be made by placing raw fish in a can and allowing it to decompose into a thick, oily substance. Doughballs soaked in this make fine catfish baits.

Two commercial dough baits on the market are Uncle Josh Carp Bait and Uncle Josh Panfish Bait.

Fish and Fish Egg Baits

Cut fish baits may be used for a variety of fish. Cut perch or pickerel belly, with or without a spinner, is a favorite for pickerel, pike, and bass. It is especially effective jigged off the bottom, or skittered over the tops of lilies or weedbeds.

A throat or belly portion of any medium-size minnow or sucker, cut to shape, is a highly effective lure for rainbow, cutthroat, brown, or Dolly Varden trout. The pectoral fin of a trout, floated down in the current of a stream, twitched and played properly, makes an effective lure for large trout.

A strip of cut smelt, sucker, or herring, trolled deep with a large spinner, makes a fine lure for lake trout or for coho or king salmon. Small pieces of cut fish make excellent baits for yellow perch, bluegills, and other sunfish.

The most popular fish egg bait is salmon eggs. Whether fresh or preserved, they rank next to worms as the favorite bait for trout. They are used singly or in clusters. To enclose a cluster of eggs, wrap them in cheese cloth and tie it at the top. This is one of the favorite baits for steelheads.

Fish eyes make one of the best baits for yellow perch, especially under the ice. After catching several perch, pop their eyes out with your thumbnail by pressing just below the eye. Use one or two eyes on a small hook, jiggle occasionally to attract the perch's attention. Fish eyes also make a good ice-fishing bait for walleyes.

Meat Baits

At one time or another, practically every kind of meat has been used as bait. The liver of various animals (beef, chicken, rabbit, pork, lamb, etc.) is a favorite bait for catfish, and sometimes for panfish like yellow perch or rock bass. Pieces of beefsteak are also good, and in strips are used extensively for pike. Left to spoil, any meat makes a good stink bait for catfish. Chicken entrails, crow, and the parts of other animals are all good. Large river catfish are sometimes caught on huge baits, such as half a spoiled rabbit or chicken.

Pork Rind

This is perhaps the most versatile and popular of all the cut baits. It can be used on every type of freshwater gamefish, either alone or in combination with spinners, spoons, flies, or lures. It is now made in a wide variety of shapes, sizes, and colors. Uncle Josh Bait Co. is the largest supplier and sells numerous pork-rind baits.

Stink Baits

Used primarily for catfish. See the section on Crustaceans, the section on Clams, for one of the best stink baits made of clams. See Blood Baits, Cheese Baits, Dough Baits in this section.

Any kind of meat allowed to spoil in the sun makes an excellent stink bait. Use spoiled minnows, frogs, chicken entrails, beef, liver, or chicken gizzards. Good stink baits are made by cutting suitable sizes of sponge rubber, and soaking them in rancid mixtures of cheese, meat, or fish.

Vegetable Baits

One of the favorite baits for trout is whole kernels of canned corn. It is highly effective on brook trout, rainbow trout, and brown trout.

A favorite vegetable bait for bullheads is peanut butter bait. Mix equal parts of peanut butter and flour moistened with hot water. Divide into balls. This is an excellent bait and it stays on the hook better than some others.

Carp can be caught on peas, lima beans, or corn. A vegetable dough of dried dog food, or bran, mixed with flour and water makes fine doughballs.

PART IV

Recommendations for Different Fishes

BROOK TROUT, BROWN TROUT, RAINBOW TROUT, CUTTHROAT TROUT

There are several good reasons for grouping these four fish together in making recommendations for lures, flies, and bait.

These four trout are the most widely distributed and sought after in the United States. Brook trout, browns, and rainbows are found from coast to coast. Cutthroat are limited to the waters of the western part of the continent, but they usually share these waters with one or more of the other three trout species; they also eat the same type of food and hit the same types of bait and artificials.

In corresponding with fish and game departments and anglers all over the United States, the author could not find any separate recommendations for any one of these four trout species. Almost the same lures, flies, and bait were used for all four species. Therefore, it seems senseless to repeat the identical recommendation in separate chapters for each of these four species.

Finally, most of the variations in lures, flies, and bait are variations from region to region rather than from fish to fish. Thus, a favorite trout fly in the Rocky Mountains is used for all species of trout in that region, but may not be used, or may be only seldom used, for any species in another region.

Dry-Fly Patterns

As mentioned in the section on dry flies, a basic assortment ought to include a variety of types and sizes as well as a variety of patterns. The suggested list below provides a variety of type, pattern, and size. Additional patterns under each type and additional sizes of each pattern can be added as resources are available.

Bivisible: Brown—#12, 14.
Divided Wing: Adams (or female Adams), Black Gnat, Blue Dun, Cahill Light, Ginger Quill, Hendrickson (dark or light), Mosquito, Quill Gordon, Royal Coachman—#10, 12, 14.
Downwing: Grasshopper Fly, Hornberg Special (see terrestrial recommendations); Muddler Minnow (see Streamer Fly recommendations).
Fanwing: Royal Coachman—#10, 14.
Hackle: Brown Hackle Peacock, Gray Hackle Yellow—#10, 16.
Hairbody: Irresistible—#10, 12.
Hairwing: Gray, Brown, Royal Wulff Flies—#8, 12. Hairwing Royal Coachman—#10, 14.
Midge: Black, Brown, Blue Dun—#20, 22.
Spider: Brown, Blue Dun, Ginger—#12, 16.
Variant: Brown, Multi-color, Red—#14.
Gauze-Wing Patterns: Any mayfly or drake listed under this category in the section on Dry Flies—#8, 10.
Parachute: Black Gnat, Cahill Dark, Cahill Light, Royal Coachman—#14.

Wet-Fly Patterns

The same principle in selecting dry flies applies in selecting wet flies: a variety of types and sizes as well as a variety of patterns.

Divided Wing: Black Gnat, Blue Dun, Coachman, Ginger Quill, Royal Coachman—#8, 10, 12. Add Coachman Leadwing, Cowdung, Gold-Ribbed Hare's Ear, Montreal, Parmacheene Belle, Western Bee (or McGinty) as money permits
Feather Wing: Cahill (Dark and Light), Professor, Quill Gordon—#8, 10, 12.
Hackle Patterns: Brown Hackle, Gray Hackle—#6, 10. Black, Yellow, Green, True's, and Black and Orange Wooly Worms—#6, 8, 10
Hairwing: Royal Coachman, McGinty, Silver Doctor—#8, 14. Picket Pin—#10

Nymphs

Recommended patterns: Black and Orange, Black and Yellow, Caddis Fly Nymphs, Gray Nymph, Green Caddis, Mayfly Nymphs (Brown, Cream, Gray, Olive, Yellow), Stonefly Nymphs (Brown and Orange), Brown and Gray, Gray and Yellow, and Tellico—#8, 12, 16.

Most nymphs may be obtained weighted or unweighted. Select some of both. Weighed nymphs may be purchased in smaller sizes than unweighted.

Streamer Flies

Select some each of feather streamers, hair streamers, and maribou streamers.

Feather Streamers: Black Ghost, Gray Ghost, Green Ghost, Parmacheene Belle, Supervisor—#6, 10.
Hair Streamers: Black and White Bucktail, Black Nosed Dace, Edson Tiger (Dark and Light), Mickey Finn, Muddler Minnow (Natural, Black and White—#4, 8, 12), Royal Coachman Bucktail, Red and White Bucktail—#8, 12.
Maribou Streamers: Black, White—#8, 12. Mylar Maribou (Gray)—#10

Terrestrials

Ants: Black, Red, Red and Black—#10, 14, 16.
Beetle: Black—#12.
Cricket: Black—#10.
Grasshopper and Hornberg: Grasshopper (Yellow, Green—#6, 10, 14), Hornberg—#8, 12.
Jassids: Black—#16, 20.

Spinning Lures

Jigs: May be used off stream bottom, allowing them to dart in current, sink to bottom again to rest.

Little Doggie Maribou Jig Fly, 1/16 oz., Black, White (Glen Evans).

Worth Jewel Head Jig, ⅛ oz., Green, Gold and Yellow colors (Worth).
Plain Jig Head, 1/16 oz., Yellow, Brown. Use with live bait, pork rind (Assassinator Lures).

Plugs: Trout, especially larger ones, will take small plugs readily. Lures are most often trolled, but may be cast.

Flatfish. Floating-diving wobbler. Fly-rod size (2″), Light Orange. Also get White (Helin).
Inch Minnow. Sinking wobbler, 1/16 oz., Silver Sides (Falls Bait Co.)
Lazy Ike. Sinking wobbler, ⅛ oz., (2″), Shad (Lazy Ike Corp.).
Rapala. Sinking wobbler, 2¾″, Silver (Normark Corp.).
Rebel Shiner Minnow. Floating diving wobbler, ⅛ oz., Purple (Norman Manufacturing Co.).
ThinFin Super Shiner Minnow. Floating-diving wobbler, 2½″ (⅛ oz.), Red (Storm Manufacturing Co.).

Spoons: Spoons are probably the best all-around casting or trolling spinning lures for trout. The following are among the best ones out of hundreds.

Al's Goldfish, ¼ oz., Rembrandt Gold (Al's Goldfish Lure Co.).
Dardevle Skeeter Plus, 1/32 oz., Black and Yellow Stripe (Lou J. Eppinger).
Dardevle Spinnie, ¼ oz., Red and White (Lou J. Eppinger).
Feathered Shad King, #2 size, Nickel/White Hackle (Hildebrandt).
Gemini Spoon, 1/30 oz., Nickel (Al's Goldfish Lure Co.).
Little Bantam, ¼ oz., Hammered Nickel (Southern Tool and Die Co.).
Little Cleo, ⅙ oz., Salmon Egg Finish/treble hook (Seneca).
Marathon Dictator Spoon, #0, ⅛ oz., Blue Mullet/Nickel (Marathon).
Mooselook Wobbler, ⅙ oz., Chrome. Also get Ivory and Red, primarily for trolling (J. A. Greene).
Phantom Wobbler, Baby, Nickel & Pearl (H & J).
Shag Spoon, ¼ oz., Pearl/Nickel (Glen L. Evans).
Slim Spoon, ¼ oz., Hammered Brass (Weber).
Williams Nymph, 1¼″ (1/40 oz.), Gold (Williams Gold Refining Co.).

Worth Wobble Spoon, ⅛ oz., Fluor, Red/Nickel (Worth).

Trolling Spinner Rigs: Use with lead line or wire line to get down deep.

1 set small spinners and keel, such as Seneca Tiny Troll (14½"), or Webertroll (12").
1 set large spinners and keel, such as Dave Davis, 3 blades (24")

These may be used with leader and hook, live bait, or lure.

Weighted Spinners: These are highly effective for trout, especially effective as casting lures.

Colorado Spinner, #1, Pearl (Horrocks-Ibbotson).
Droppen, ⅛ oz., Black Blade, Gold Body (Garcia).
Hep Spinner, Squirrel tail, 1/16 oz., Gold (Daisy-Heddon).
Mepps Aglia, #0 (1/12 oz.), Plain, Red and White blade (Sheldon's, Inc.).
Mepps Aglia Long, #1 (⅙ oz.), Plain, Blue Blade (Sheldon's).
Mepps Comet, #3 (⅕ oz.) with Silver Blade, plastic mino (Sheldon's).
Panther Martin, #1/16 oz., regular, silver blade, yellow/Red Body (Harrison-Hoge).
Prescott Nipigon Cockatoush, #4 hook, White on Black body (Prescott).
Shyster Spinner, 1/16 oz., Brass blade, Orange and Black Spotted Body (Glen Evans).

Bait

Cheese (hunks or in dough)
Corn
Crawfish
Crickets (late summer)
Cut-fish strip (with spinner)
Grasshoppers (late summer)
Mayfly larvae
Marshmallows (small)
Minnows (small), for still-fishing, live or sewn for trolling
Nightcrawlers or earthworms
Salmon eggs
Stonefly nymphs

DOLLY VARDEN, GOLDEN, AND GRAYLING TROUT

These three trout have nothing at all in common except that they are not as widely distributed as those discussed in the previous chapter. Recommendations for each of these three species will be given separately.

DOLLY VARDEN TROUT

These trout are highly cannibalistic and so are not planted as widely as other trout. They live in both cold streams and in lakes of the Rocky Mountains and Pacific Northwest. The emphasis in the selection of artificials or bait ought to be on those which represent other fish. Thus, they will readily take a wide variety of spoons and spinners. Streamer flies are a favorite type of fly, although dries, wets, and nymphs may be used occasionally in streams. The bait fisherman need not be fussy: fish bait (cut) and salmon eggs are favorites, along with worms. The specific recommendations are as follows:

Flies

Any of the streamers in the previous chapter are the preferred type of fly. Of the terrestrials, the grasshopper and Hornberg are good in late summer in streams. Dries, wets, and nymphs may be used in streams as the situation demands it, selecting from those patterns listed in the previous section which are local favorites or which "match the hatch."

Jigs, Plugs, Spoons, Weighted Spinners

Any of those suggested in the previous section are good.

Bait

Cut bait: Cut sucker, minnow throat or belly.
Pork rind strips: Use with spinners, flies, spoons.
Minnows: Use stillfishing or trolling.
Salmon eggs: Singly or in clusters.
Worms or nightcrawlers.

GOLDEN TROUT

These fish are a fly fisherman's delight, since insects are their principal food supply. They can be unpredictable and difficult to catch, however, so the fisherman will have to learn to be patient to find them feeding. The best flies are small sizes, #12–22, with tiny midge flies often best. Small dries work well when the fish are surfacing for food; caddis nymphs are the favorite underwater flies. Streamers, small spinners, or spoons will sometimes take large fish. The following assortment should give the fisherman enough variety to meet most conditions.

Dry Flies

Bivisible: Black, Brown, Grizzly—#14, 16
Divided wing: Adams, Black Gnat, Blue Dun, Ginger Quill, Quill Gordon, Royal Coachman, White Miller —#12–18
Midges: Adams, Black, Blue Dun, Brown, Cream, Olive —#20, 22
Spider: Black, Blue, Ginger—#16, 18

Wet Flies

Divided Wing: Adams, Coachman, Gold-Ribbed Hare's Ear, Rio Grande King—#10–14
Feather Wing: Professor—#12
Hackle: Gray Hackle—#14

Nymphs

Black Midge
Caddis Fly Nymph
Green Caddis
Gray Nymph
Shrimp (translucent, natural, pink, and red) #14, 16

Streamers

These are not often used, but the angler ought to have several just in case: #10, 12.

Feather Streamers: Black Ghost, Gray Ghost, Royal Coachman
Hair Streamers: Black Nosed Dace, Edson Tiger Dark, Mickey Finn, Muddler Minnow
Maribou Streamers: Black, White

Terrestrials

Ants: Black, Red—#14, 16.
Grasshopper and Hornberg: Yellow, or Green grasshopper, Hornberg—#12, 14
Jassid: Black—#16

Spinners

Marathon Kat-Claw, 3/32 oz., Nickel Blade/Copper body
Mepps Black Fury, 1/8 oz., Plain
Worth Pearlette, 1/32 oz. (#12, 14 hook)
Worth Spinette, 1/16 oz. (#10 hook), Hammered Brass Blade

Spoons

Abalone Demon, 1/5 oz. (Worth)
Abu-Toby, 1/4 oz., Silver/Red (Garcia)
Weber Spoons, 1/8 oz., Hammered Brass, Red and White/Brass, or Red/Brass (Weber)
Williams Thinfish, 1/8 oz., Gold Mirror (Williams Gold Refining Co.)

Bait

Caddis worms
Freshwater shrimp
Grasshoppers (late summer)
Salmon eggs
Worms or nightcrawlers

GRAYLING TROUT

Grayling are the dry-fly angler's dream, since they rise eagerly to dries. They will readily take wet flies, nymphs, and streamers as well, but these are less frequently used since the fish can be caught so easily on dries. Small spoons, spinners, and live bait may also be used, but usually are not used as often as flies. Grayling have a small mouth so flies should be size #12 or smaller. Spoons and spinners should be of the smallest sizes convenient to use. The following should give the angler a fine assortment for all occasions.

Dry Flies

Bivisibles: Badger, Brown—#14
Divided Wing: Adams, Black Gnat, Blue Dun, Blue Quill, Cahill (Light or Dark), Hendrickson Light, March Brown, Olive Dun, Quill Gordon—#12 and #16
Hackle: Brown Hackle, Gray Hackle Peacock—#16
Hairwing: Gray Wulff, Royal Wulff—#12
Midge: Black, Brown—#20
Variant: Red Variant—#16

Wet Flies

Divided Wing: Coachman, Cowdung, Rio Grande King, Royal Coachman, Stonefly—#12
Feather Wing: Cahill Dark, Grizzly King, Queen of Waters

Nymphs

Black and Yellow	Black Midge
Black and Orange	Gray Nymph
#16	

Streamer Flies

Hair Streamers: Black Nosed Dace, Brown and White Bucktail, Gray Squirrel Red, Royal Coachman Bucktail
Feather Streamers: Barnes Special, Black Demon, Cain's River, Black Ghost, Grizzly King
Maribou Streamers: White

Terrestrials

Black Flying Ant—#20	Jassids—Black, Yellow—#18

Spinners

Since flies are used much more frequently, only three will suffice.

Hectic Spinner, ⅛ oz., Plain, Polished Nickel (Glen Evans)
Worden's Rooster Tail, 1/16 oz., Gray (Yakima Bait Co.)
Worth Blitz Spinner, 1/12 oz., Plain, Brass

Spoons

A few basic spoons should meet most needs.

Heritage, 3/16 oz., Red and White/Nickel (Daisy-Heddon)
Johnson's Sprite, ⅛ oz., Gold (Louis Johnson)
Phantom Wobbler, Baby, Nickel and Pearl (H & J)
Sidewinder, ⅛ oz., Nickel/Neon Blue (Seneca)
Super Duper, ⅙ oz., Red Head (Gladding—South Bend)

LAKE TROUT

The lake trout is an extremely cold-water fish, preferring water temperatures of from 40 to 45 degrees. For this reason, it is caught in shallow water during summer months only in the extremely cold-water lakes of the far North, and in other lakes in the cold water of early spring for several weeks after ice out, or in the late fall, usually during spawning time. Lures must be fished where the fish are. This means deep trolling gear when the surface temperatures are too warm, and shallow-running lures or flies only in the spring or late fall.

The primary lures for lake trout are wobbling spoons. Secondarily, they will hit wobbling plugs, spinners, or jigging spoons. When the fish are shallow, streamer flies, or even a few dry flies may be added to this list. Of course, live bait is always good if fished at whatever depths the fish are.

Casting or Trolling Spoons

The fisherman should have a small assortment of sizes, finishes, and types. The following list includes some very fine ones.

Abu-Kaster, 5/8 oz., Silver Scale (Garcia Corp)
Abu-Toby, 3/8 oz., Silver/Red (Garcia)
Chev. Chase, 1/3 oz., Fluor. Orange (Chev Chase Lures)
Cop-E-Cat Jr., 1 oz., Blue Herring Scale (Lou Eppinger)
Doctor Spoon, 5/8 oz., Gold (Prescott Spinner Co.)
Geneva Spoon, 3", Chrome, single hook (Arthur Freer)
K-B Spoon, 1/4 oz., Copper (Prescott)
Koho Devle, 1 1/4 oz., Red and White Stripe/Nickel (Lou Eppinger)
Lake Clear Wobbler, 3 1/4", Two-tone Chrome and Brass, with single snelled hook for live bait (Arthur Freer)

Marathon Rattle Spoon, ¼ oz., Red and Yellow Stripe/ Nickel (Marathon)
Mooselook Wobbler, ⅙ oz., Ivory and Red (J. A. Greene)—a real killer, try it
Paul Bunyan Flash Eye Spoon, ½ oz., #5/0 weedless hook, Gold (Prescott Spinner Co.)
Phantom Wobbler, Senior, Copper (H and J Fishing Tackle)
Red-Eye Wiggler, 1 oz., Speckled (Hofschneider Corp)
Rok't-Devle Imp., ⅘ oz. (Very heavy weight for size), 2¼", Brass (Lou Eppinger)
Tony Accetta Pet Spoon, feathered model (Red), Chrome, ½ oz. (Tony Accetta)
Twin-Fin, 3", Gold (Pcola'a)
Voyager, ⅙ oz., Pearl Luster Rainbow (Daisy-Heddon)
Williams Wobblers, ½ oz., Half and Half Nu-rinkle (Williams Gold Refining Co.)

Jigging Spoons

Some of the above, especially those with single hooks, may be used for jigging. In addition, here are some other spoons meant primarily for jigging, with or without bait attached.

Flying Fin, 1¾", Chrome (H & J)
Johnson's Lucky Lujon, 1 oz., Brass (Louis Johnson Co.)
Laker Spoon (Russian Hook), #2 hook, Hammered Brass (Best Tackle Co.)

Trolling Rigs

Any of the larger, longer trolling rigs listed in the section on Spinners. Or, some fishermen prefer a single large spinner (up to 6" or 8" long). The deeper the fishing, the larger the spinners should be.

Weighted Spinners

Bead Ghost, No. 100, 2¼" blade, White & Orange Blade (Best)
Mepps Giant Killer, with Mino, 1½ oz., Silver Blade/ Red Dots (Sheldon's, Inc.)
Mepps Aglia Long, ½ oz., White Bucktail, Fluor, Red Blade (Sheldon's, Inc.)

Plugs

Walpala Cisco Kid, 7/32 oz., 3½" long, Burgundy Silver (Cisco Kid Tackle)
Finn-Oreno, 3/8 oz. (5⅛"), Silver Green (Gladding-South Bend)
Flatfish, No. 5, 4", Red Fluorescent (Helin)
Tadpolly, ½ oz., Red Head Flitter (Daisy-Heddon)

Jigs

Jigging Rapala, ½ oz. (2¾"), Silver (Normark Corp.)

Bait

Live minnows, smelt, suckers
Cut smelt, herring, minnows, suckers with spoon or spinners
Sewn bait: Minnows, smelt for use in trolling with spinners

Streamer Flies

Generally brighter colors: red, white, yellow are best.

Alaska Mary Ann
Black Ghost
Blonde Bucktails
Golden Darter
Gov. Aiken
Mickey Finn
Mylar Silver Shiner
Parmacheene Belle
Red and White Bucktail
Royal Coachman
White Maribou

Sizes 1/0, 1, 2, 4

KOKANEE, LANDLOCKED AND OUANANICHE SALMON

Kokanee is a landlocked dwarf form of the Pacific sockeye salmon. The term landlocked, at least in the East, refers to landlocked Atlantic salmon. The ouananiche is really identical to the landlocked Atlantic, but it lives only in Quebec, Labrador, and Newfoundland.

KOKANEE

Other than it also is a landlocked fish, the kokanee has nothing in common with the landlocks of the East. Because it feeds primarily on plankton, it is regarded by anglers as difficult to catch. There are three primary methods used to catch this fish.

1. Handlining with bait—daytime, or night with lantern on boat or dock.
2. Trolling deep with large spinners, flashers and bait (occasionally spoons).
3. Snagging by using a bare treble hook along the bottom.

When the fish are on the surface, they may be caught on occasion with small flies.

Bait

The favorite baits are worms, maggots, corn, salmon eggs on a plain hook.

Trolling Rigs

When the fish are deep, use large flashing spinners (see the section on Spinners—Trolling Spinner Rigs) on wire or lead-core line with leader to which is attached a single hook with bait, or occasionally a wobbling spoon.

Lures

Any of the wobbling spoons recommended in the section on Spoons will do, but they must be small, about 3 inches maximum. The reader ought to know that actually artificial lures are seldom used for this fish; bait is the favorite. A cherry bobber trolled deep is used to some extent.

Flies

Kokanee are fond of surfacing and may sometimes be caught with flies, usually on rare occasions. Select several small patterns, sizes #10–16, either dry or wet, for such times.

LANDLOCKED AND OUANANICHE SALMON

These will be considered together since both are landlocked Atlantic salmon and are caught by identical methods.

Superb sporting fish, they may be caught by almost every method: flies (dry, wet, streamers, nymphs); lures (plugs, spoons, spinners); live bait (casting or trolling). It's a toss-up whether streamer flies or spoons are favorites, but there are probably more trollers for landlocked salmon than there are casters. This fish prefers water temperatures of around 50 degrees, so the fishermen may often have to go deep with lead or wire line in the summer. However, even during warm months the salmon rise to the surface to feed in early morning and evening and may be caught by casting or trolling flies or spoons during these periods.

The salmon are also found in some rivers and streams throughout the year, and in many more in the spring and fall, where they may be caught with conventional fly casting and spinning methods. At such times, they may rise readily to the dry fly, or take a small wet fly, nymph, or streamer.

Wobbling Spoons

Al's Goldfish, ¼ oz., Gold and Rembrandt Gold are both excellent (Al's Goldfish Lure Co.)
Dardevle Spinnie, ¼ oz., Red and White/Nickel (Lou Eppinger)
Mooselook Wobbler, ⅙ oz., Chrome, Ivory and Red are the two best with Fluor. Orange occasionally needed (J. A. Greene). This lure is the best all-around trolling lure as far as I am concerned
Otterget Lure, ⅙ oz., White/Red Spots or Smelt finish (Otterget Lure Co.)
Phantom Wobbler, Junior Size. Pearl and Pink/Nickel or /Copper (J. A. Greene). One of the best for trolling or casting
Sidewinder, ⅕ oz., Nickel or Gold/Neon Red. Primarily for river casting, since it will not twist line in the fastest current (Seneca Tackle)
Super-Duper, ¼ oz., Red Head or Chrome. Best used in river or stream fishing in fast water (Gladding-South Bend)
Williams Thinfish, ¼ oz., Half and Half (gold and silver) Mirror (Williams Gold Refining Co.)

Plugs

Deep-Dive Tiger, ¼ oz., sinking model, Silver (Daisy-Heddon)
Flatfish, Expert Jr., 2½", floating model, Light Orange/Red Head, or White/Red Head Black Top (Helin)
Lazy Ike, ⅕ oz. (1¾"), Metallic Purple, sinking lure (Lazy Ike Corp.)
Rapala, 3½", Silver, floating model (Normark Corp.)
Rascal, ¼ oz. (1¾"), Gold (Gladding-South Bend)
Rebel, Deep Runner Minnow, ½ oz., with plastic bill, floats, dives deep, Blue or Red Eye (Norman)

Spinners, Weighted Spinners

Spinners are most often used as part of a trolling rig. Dave Davis (either 2,3, or 5 blades) are favorites in New England. Weighted spinner lures are seldom used; most fishermen prefer wobbling spoons. However, for casting, especially in streams and rivers, the weighted spinner lures are good producers, although line twist will sometimes be a problem with some lures. Use any of the Mepps type with weighted spinners, plain treble hooks, sizes 1/8 or 1/4 ounce.

Streamer Flies

Black Ghost
Brown and White Bucktail
Edson Tiger, Dark
Gov. Aiken
Gray Ghost
Green Ghost
Little Brook Trout
Little Rainbow Trout
Mickey Finn
Mylar Ghosts: Gray, Green, White
Red and White Bucktail
Supervisor
White Maribou

Sizes 2, 4, 6, 8, 12. Some fishermen prefer tandem hooks in the large sizes for trolling.

Dry Flies

Black Midge—#20, 22
Brown Bivisible—#12
Brown Hackle—#14
Brown Wulff—#10, 12
Gray Hackle—#14
Gray Wulff—#10, 12
White Wulff—#10, 16

Also, get Blue Dun, or Yellow Gauze Wing Drake, #10, 12 (Phillips)

Terrestrials

Dry Fly Ant, #16, 20. Get Black and Cinnamon colors (Orvis)
Perfect Ant, #12, 14, Red and Black, Black. Fish it wet (Phillips)
Jassid, #18, Black. Fish semi-wet, just under the surface film (Dan Bailey)

Nymphs

Primarily for stream and river fishing.

Black Midge—#14 etc. (Orvis)
Caddis Fly—#10 (Dan Bailey)
Gray Nymph—#8, 12 (Dan Bailey)
Green Caddis—#12 (Orvis)
Mayfly Nymphs—#10, 12, 16 (Dan Bailey)—Black, Cream, Gray, Tan, Yellow
Stonefly Nymphs—#6, 8, 10, Black and Orange (Orvis), and Gray and Yellow (Dan Bailey)

Bait

Nightcrawlers: Use stillfishing, stream fishing, or trolling with large spinners, either shallow or with deep-running gear.
Smelt: Live—stillfishing or sewn on trolling gear.
Shiner Minnows: Primarily used sewn on trolling gear.

ARCTIC CHAR, INCONNU OR SHEEFISH, AND SEA TROUT (SEA-RUN BROWNS)

These three fish are all anadromous (those which live in salt water and ascend freshwater rivers to spawn). The arctic char is found in the northern waters of both oceans: Alaska and northern Canada in the Pacific and Greenland and Iceland (among others) in the Atlantic. It occurs also in smaller landlocked forms in some lakes.

Inconnu, or sheefish, are found only in the waters of Alaska in the United States, and are common in northern Canadian waters along the Pacific. Sea trout (sea-run browns) are found in a few waters of the U.S. only in the East, and some eastern

Canadian waters, as well as waters of Newfoundland, Iceland, and those of many other countries bordering the Atlantic ocean.

All three fish will take wobbling spoons and spinners. They may also be caught with flies, especially bright-colored streamer fly and wet salmon fly and steelhead patterns. The recommendations below include a varied assortment of wobbling spoons, weighted spinners, and flies. Landlocked arctic char, which run much smaller than their anadromous relatives, may be taken also with any standard dry-fly patterns. Sea trout are often taken with dry flies in Norway, England, and other countries where they occur, but not often with dries in countries where they are found along our side of the Atlantic.

Wobbling Spoons

Abalone Demon, 1/5 oz., Abalone/Chrome (Worth)
Dardevlet, 3/5 oz., Red and White/Nickel (Lou Eppinger)
Johnson's Sprite, 3/4 oz., Gold (Louis Johnson)
Marathon Dictator Spoon, 5/8 oz., Hammered Copper (Marathon)
Mr. Champ, 1/2 oz., Silver color/White Bucktail (Weber)
Mooselook Wobbler, 3/8 oz., Chrome or Fluor. Orange (J. A. Greene)
Seneca Salmon, 3/4 oz., Nickel (Seneca)
Tony's Spoon, 3/8 oz., Chrome/Red streamer (Tony Accetta)
Weber Spoon, Magnum (Heavy Metal), 5/8 oz., Flor. Red/Brass (Weber)
Williams Whitefish, 1 oz., Silver Mirror (Williams Gold Refining Co.)

Weighted Spinners

Hectic Spinner, 1/3 oz., Hammered Brass (Glen Evans)
Mepps Aglia Long, 1/2 oz., Gold (Sheldon's, Inc.)

Mepps Giant Killer, 1 oz., Gold/Red Dots, plain (Sheldon's)
Mitchell, ¼ oz., Silver Body/Silver and Black Striped Blade (Garcia)
The Prowler, ¼ oz., White and Red (Best Tackle)
Worth Blitz, ½ oz., Plain Nickel (Worth)

Flies

Wet Flies

Black Doctor (Atlantic salmon fly)
Blue Charm (Atlantic salmon fly)
Carson (steelhead fly)
Golden Demon (steelhead fly)
Railbird (steelhead fly)
Silver Doctor (Atlantic salmon fly)
Silver Wilkerson (Atlantic salmon fly)
Thor (steelhead fly)

Sizes 2, 4, 6

European Sea-Trout Patterns

Black Pennel
Bloody Butcher
Blue Zulu
Mallard and Claret
Peter Ross
Silver March Brown
Teal and Green
Teal and Yellow

Sizes 2, 4, 6
Note: These patterns are not described elsewhere in this book.

Streamer Flies

Use mylar body bucktail streamer flies (Dan Bailey) in the following patterns:

Brown-Blue-Yellow
Brown and White
Integration (Black and White)
Mickey Finn
Red and White
Silver Doctor

Sizes 1/0, 1, 4

ATLANTIC SALMON

On the North American continent, fishing for this fish is limited to fly fishing. It is caught primarily on especially developed patterns of wet flies. However, dry flies are being used more and more, especially the hairflies.

A small assortment for use in North America should include all of the following in sizes 1/0–10.

- Black Dose
- Blue Charm
- Conrad
- Durham Ranger
- Dusty Miller
- Green Highlander
- Jock Scott
- Silver Doctor
- Silver Gray
- Silver Rat
- Thunder and Lightning

As money becomes available, buy other Atlantic salmon patterns listed in the section on Salmon and Steelhead flies. The larger sizes are used early in the season in high water; the smaller sizes in late summer in low water.

Dry Flies

- Brown Bivisible
- Brown Hackle
- Cinnamon Sedge
- Deadly McIntosh
- Gray Hackle
- Pink Hackle
- Salmon Irresistible (Orvis Co.)
- Wulff Flies: Black, brown, gray, grizzly, royal, white

Sizes 6–12

These flies are most effective in low water. Atlantic Salmon have been caught on dries in small sizes (as small as #16), but the sizes selected above should do for most purposes.

STEELHEAD TROUT

Steelhead are rainbow trout which descend Pacific coastal rivers to live briefly in the ocean and then return to those rivers to spawn. Runs occur almost year-round in some rivers, with peak periods of the summer and winter runs varying from river to river. Winter steelheads run the rivers when the water is high, and sometimes roily, and so are harder to reach, particularly with the flyrod. However, with the advent of weighted shooting heads and torpedo lines, many fishermen are successfully fly fishing for steelheads during the winter months as well as during the summer. Steelheads are caught with bait, artificial spoons, spinners and plugs, both trolling and casting.

Flies

Favorite fly patterns vary from region to region, river to river, and with the time of year. Flies which have been developed especially for steelhead are sparsely dressed with large, heavy hooks, allowing the fly to sink readily. Some of the Atlantic salmon patterns are also used for steelheads and vice-versa (both are dressed on large, heavy hooks).

Dry flies are sometimes used for summer steelheads in low water. Some traditional trout streamers and wet flies are also used on steelhead, as well as a few dry trout patterns.

Steelhead Patterns (Tied Wet)

Babine Special
Boss
Burlap
Coles Comet
Cummings Special
Doctor Rex
Fall Favorite
Golden Demon
Hoyts Killer
Jock Scott
Kalema Special
Marietta
McLeod Ugly
Orange Demon
Polar Shrimp
Purple Peril
Rogue River Special
Royal Coachman
Silver Doctor
Silver Hilton
Skunk
Skykomish Sunrise
Thor
Umpqua Special
Yellow Hammer

Sizes 6–1/0 assorted

As money allows, additional patterns might be added from the list in the chapter on Salmon and Steelhead Flies.

Dry Flies For Steelhead

These should be tied with hair such as polar bear, caribou, or bucktail. Probably the most often used are the Wulff flies: black, brown, gray, royal, sizes 4–8. In addition to these, add:

Irresistible: (with salmon hook), #4–#8
Bucktail Caddis–green, yellow, orange–#6–#10 (Dan Bailey)
Kolzer Firefly Dry Flies–red, yellow, orange–#8–#10 (Dan Bailey)
Sofa Pillow, #4–#8 (Dan Bailey)

A Few Trout Patterns Sometimes Used on Steelhead

Jock Scott, Royal Coachman, Silver Doctor–already on the list of steelhead flies
Black Gnat, Coachman, Gray Hackle Yellow, Grizzly King, Mickey Finn Bucktail, Professor

Plugs

Flatfish, underwater model, either 3¼″ or 2⅝″, Red Fluor, or Luminous Orange Scale (Helin)

Gay Blade, ¼ oz., Rainbow or Golden Shiner (Cordell)
Hot Shot, 1/10 oz. or ¼ oz., Fluor. Red or Yellow (Eddie Pope)
Tiny River Runt Spook, ¼ oz., sinking, Red Head (Daisy-Heddon)
Will's Original Cherry Bobber, #4–#10, treble hook (Glen Evans)
Will's Sammy Special, Pink Body/Pink Streamer (Glen Evans)
Wobble-Glo Lures, ¾" body, Flame Orange (Yakima Bait Co.)
Worden's Spin-N-Glo, sizes ½"–1", Flame and Chartreuse, Pearl Clown, or Flame Orange colors (Yakima Bait Co.)

Spinners

Mepps Aglia Long, #3, ⅓ oz., Gold or Fluor. Red blade (Sheldon's, Inc.)
Rainbow Cluster, #6 hook, weighted (Worth)
Worden's Rooster Tail, #5, ⅜ oz., Fluor. Pink (Yakima)

Spoons

Heavyweight metal is preferred to enable the angler to get down deep.

Dardevle Rok't Devle Imp., ⅘ oz., Red and White/Nickel (Lou Eppinger)
Hot Shot Wobbler, ¼ oz. or ⅜ oz., Gold Fluor. Stripe (Eddie Pope)
Wobble-L-Rite, ⅝ oz., Hammered Brass or Hammered Nickle (Seneca)
Worth Casting Spoons, Heavyweight, 1¾" (Worth) Fluor. Orange and White/Nickel back or Fluor. Red and White/Copper back, or Fluor. Orange/Brass Stripe

Bait

Salmon eggs, or steelhead eggs, fresh or preserved. Put up in clusters, usually in cheesecloth sacks. These are the most important bait used.

Nightcrawlers or worms are used to some extent.

PACIFIC SALMON

Pacific Salmon along the North American continent include the following:

Chinook, or king, salmon
Chum, or dog, salmon
Coho, or silver, salmon
Humpback, or pink, salmon
Sockeye salmon

Of these five species, chinook and coho salmon are the only important sport species. Chum salmon and sockeyes are only rarely taken by sport fishermen, humpback, or pink, salmon are taken fairly frequently, usually while trolling offshore for kings or cohos. Since many of the methods and lures are similar for both kings and cohos, these species will be considered together, with differences indicated when important.

Bait

The bait fisherman offshore and in river estuaries usually uses herring as his bait, but with candlefish used to a lesser extent. Herring are sewn on whole, headless, or as a strip cut from the side, with one treble hook, a treble and single hook, or two single hooks used in the sewing. If the bait is put on bent, it will spin when retrieved (this method is called spinning). A herring dodger, or large metal flasher which moves from side to side, is sometimes used between a heavy sinker (2–6 ounces) and the bait when trolling.

Herring are fished from an anchored boat by stripping (casting the bait out with loose coils of line at one's feet, letting the bait sink to the bottom, and, after an interval, stripping the line back in) and by mooching (trolling the herring along or near the bottom from a moving boat). Another method known as dead spinning involves resting the rod against the side of the anchored boat and allowing the bait to work just off the bottom where the tide is working and swirling.

Other baits for kings and cohos include:

Worms and nightcrawlers, which are used primarily in inland lakes for cohos in conjunction with trolling rigs of flashing spinners. (Kings are sometimes caught along spawning routes with this rig.)

Live minnows, which are used in inland lakes like herring are in the ocean.

Salmon egg clusters or *steelhead egg clusters* (*strawberries*) are used most often in river fishing.

Spoons

Three most often used spoons include:

Dardevlet, 3/5 oz.; Dardevle, 1 oz.; and Cop-E-Cat, Jr., 1 oz. (Lou Eppinger)
Johnson's Sprite, 1/2 or 3/4 oz., (Louis Johnson)
Little Cleo, 1/4, 1/3, 2/5, 2/3, or 3/4 oz. (Seneca)

Other fine ones include:

Coho-Sur-R-Min-O, 5/8 oz. (Al's Goldfish Lure Co.)
Marathon Coho Wobbler, 1/8, 1/4, 5/8 oz. (Marathon)
Williams Wobbler, 1/4, 1/2, 3/4, 1 oz. (Williams Gold Refining Co.)

Most popular finishes are: Blue, silver, chrome, nickel, fiery red, blue and silver, red and white, and red and silver.

Spinners

The following is a fine assortment of types and colors and is especially excellent for coho salmon.

Abu-Reflex, ¾ oz., Chrome/Blue body and Chrome/Blue blade (Garcia)
Bear Valley Spinner, #2 to #4 with 3/0 to 5/0 hook
Hep, ⅜ oz., Gold finish (Daisy-Heddon)
Marathon Coho Hooker, #4 spinners, Brass/Red Skirt (Marathon)
Mepps Aglia, ½ oz., Red and White Blade. Plain hook (Sheldon's)
Shyster Spinner, ⅓ oz., Yellow/Black Stripes (Glen Evans)
Toni Spinner, ⅜ oz., Red Fluor. (Daisy-Heddon)
Worden's Rooster Tail, ¼ oz., Flame (Yakima Bait Co.)

Plugs

Big Dig, Little Big Dig (½ or ⅓ oz.), Baitfish Blue (Burke)
Flatfish, Underwater Model, 2⅝", Red Fluorescent (Helin)
Lazy Ike, ¼ oz. (2½"), Metallic Red (Lazy Ike Corp.)
L & S Mirrolure, Sinker, ¼ oz., Green Back, White Belly, Silver Scale (L & S Bait Co.)
Pikie Minnow, ½ oz., Red Head (Creek Chub)
Rapala, 3½", Silver (Normark Corp)
Rebel Shiner Minnow, ½ oz., Gold (Norman)
Tadpolly, ½ oz., Nickel Plated Blue Scale (Daisy-Heddon)
Will's Cherry Bobber, #6 treble hook (Glen Evans)

Flies

Flies are seldom used for king salmon in ocean trolling, but are sometimes used in river fishing. They are a favorite for coho salmon, in the ocean, inland lakes and in rivers. Cohos surface frequently and can be caught on large streamers at this time. Saltwater streamers are used most frequently: those with bucktail or polar bear hair and tinsel bodies. The following are recommended.

Blonde Bucktail Flies (Hank's Deadly Blonds)
Co.: Hank Roberts Outfitters
Sizes: 3/0, 2/0, 1/0, or 1
Patterns: Honey (Yellow), Platinum (White), Pink (Red and White), Strawberry (Red).

Mylar Body Bucktail Streamer Flies
Co.: Dan Bailey
Sizes: 3/0, 1/0, 2
Patterns: Brown-blue-yellow, Brown-green-white, Red and White, Silver Doctor.

Other popular patterns for salmon but which are not described in this book include: Coronation (blue, red, white), Candlefish, Coho Special, Silver Killer (green, red, white), Blue and White, Green and White. All of these have silver tinsel bodies and should be hook size #3/0 to #1. Spinners are sometimes used ahead of the fly.

BLACK BASS

There are more lures designed specifically for bass than for any other freshwater gamefish. It is important that the angler have a variety of type, color, action, and size. Therefore, in making recommendations, selections have been made from different types of surface lures, floating-diving lures, sinking lures, spoons, spinners, bass bugs, flies, and bait. A variety of finishes have been suggested, as well as different actions and sizes. Obviously, there are dozens of other good ones in addition to the recommendations which follow, but the list below has been compiled after careful listing of favorites from all over the country. The resultant list will enable the angler to meet practically all situations he encounters in bass fishing.

Surface Plugs

Plunkers, Poppers, Chuggers

Creek Chub Plunker, ½ oz., Pikie or Perch finish (Creek Chub)
Baby Chugger Spook, ⅜ oz., Black and White Shore (Daisy-Heddon)
Hula Popper, ⅝ oz., Coach Dog (Fred Arbogast)
Weedless Spin Popper, ¼ oz., Frog finish (Phillips Fly and Tackle Co.)

Sputterers

Sputterbug, ¼ oz., Red Head (Fred Arbogast)

Stick Lures

Devil's Warhorse, Top Water, ½ oz., Silver Shiner (Jack Smithwick)

Swimming Animal Lures

Crazy Crawler, Tiny, ¼ oz., Yellow/Red Head (Daisy-Heddon)
Jitterbug, ⅜ oz., Black (for night), Perch (for day) (Fred Arbogast)

Torpedo Lures

L & S Mirrolure (Surface Runner), 7M Series, ⅜ oz., Blue Back-white belly-silver scale (L & S Bait Co.)

Wounded Minnow Lures

Boy Howdy, ⅜ oz., spinner front and rear, Silver Flash (Cordell)
Skip-N-Cisco, ¼ oz., spinner aft, Red Head (Cisco Kid)
Tiny Torpedo, ¼ oz., Yellow Shore (Daisy-Heddon)

Floating Diving Plugs

Darters

Lucky 13, Baby, ⅜ oz., Perch (Daisy-Heddon)

Deep Divers

Bomber, ½ oz., White (Bomber Bait Co.)
Hellbender, ¼ oz., Yellow/Black Dots (Whopper Stopper)
Rebel, Deep Runner Minnow, ½ oz., Silver (Norman)

Wobblers

Creek Chub Pikie Minnow, ½ oz., Pikie (Creek Chub)
Flatfish, Spinning Surface, 2½", Frog (Helin)
L & S Bass-Master, ⅜ oz., White Belly/Black Back/ Speckles (L & S Bait Co.)
Meadow Mouse, ½ oz., Gray (Daisy-Heddon)
Rascal, ⅛ oz., Purple (Gladding-South Bend)
Red Fin, ⅜ oz., Golden Shiner (Cordell)
ThinFin Super Shiner Minnow, ¼ oz., Red (Storm)
Tiny River Runt Spook, ¼ oz., Red Head Flitter (Daisy-Heddon)

Sinking Plugs

Deep Divers

Devil's Horse, Deep Runner, ½ oz., Green Minnow (Jack Smithwick)
Tadpolly, ½ oz., Red Head (Daisy-Heddon)

Vibrators

Bayou Boogie, ⅓ oz., Blue Back/Silver Scale (Whopper Stopper)

Wobblers

Big Inch, ⅛ oz., Orange Tiger (Falls Bait Co.)
Diamond Jim, ½ oz., Black Knight (Al's Goldfish Lure Co.)
Hot Shot, ⅝ oz., White/Black Head (Eddie Pope)
Lazy Ike, ¼ oz., Brown Scale (Lazy Ike)
Rapala, 4⅜", Silver (Normark)

Spoons

Dardevle Spinnie, ¼ oz., Red and White/Nickel (Lou Eppinger)
Johnson's Silver Minnow, Gold, ½ oz. (Louis Johnson)
Little Bantam, ¼ oz., Hammered Nickle (Southern Tool & Die Co.)

Spinners

Abu-Reflex, 1/4 oz., White Body/Zebra Blade (Garcia)
Hawaiian Wiggler, 1/4 oz., Deep Runner, Red Head (Fred Arbogast)
Herb's Dilly, 1/4 oz., Frog and Yellow (Glen Evans)
Mepp's Black Fury, 1/6 oz., Yellow Hair (Sheldon's)
Paul Bunyan "66", 1/4 oz., Red (Prescott)
Shimmy Wiggler, 3/8 oz., Red and White (Weber)
Shyster, 1/8 oz., Brass Blade, Orange and Black (Glen Evans)
Snagless Sally, 1/2 oz., Nickel Spinner, Black-White (Hildebrandt)
Worth Blitz, 3/8 oz., Hammered Nickel Spinner (Worth)

Safety Pin Lures

Bushwhacker, 1/4 oz., Single Spinner, White/Black Dots (Bomber)
Shannon Twin Spinner, 1/4 oz., Red (Shannon Lure Co.)

Jigs

Jig'l Fly, 1/8 oz., Maribou, Pink/White (Arndt & Son)
Plain Jig Head, 1/4 oz., Black Head. For use with bait, pork rind, plastic worms or eels (Asassinator Lures).

Nature Lures

Plastic Worms, Nightcrawlers. These are the favorite and probably the most effective of all bass lures across the United States. However, they are much more effective on largemouth than on smallmouth; plastic or rubber frogs and crawfish are more effective on smallmouth. Buy both 6″ and 8″ worms. The favorite colors are purple, black, red, natural, blue and green in about that order of popularity, with purple the most popular. Professionals rig their own worms, usually with a single hook (plain or weedless) and a sliding bullet sinker on the line, or by baiting them on a single hook jig head.

Amphibians—Plastic or rubber frogs are one of the very best lures for both largemouth and smallmouth bass. Lizards and salamanders are both excellent, especially for largemouth.

Crawfish—Excellent, especially for smallmouth bass.

Eels—These rank second in popularity (nightcrawlers are first) and they are especially popular in fishing for largemouth. Black eels on a jig are excellent.

Minnows—Plastic minnows are useful, especially with a weighted spinner. They are sometimes used trolling, as well as casting.

Bait

Baitfish—Minnows, shad, alewifes, suckers, and eels (Minnows are the most popular of all baitfish.)

Nightcrawlers—Good bass bait but hard to keep on the hook where there are a lot of small panfish to steal your bait.

Hellgrammites—Especially popular bait for smallmouths.

Crawfish—Excellent for smallmouth especially.

Frogs—One of the best and most productive for both largemouth and smallmouth.

Salamanders—Very popular in some locales, especially for largemouth bass.

Pork Rind

Pork strips, skirts are highly effective when used on spinners, spoons, flies for both largemouth and smallmouth.

Pork Chunks—frog chunk is one of the very best lures for all bass, especially when used skittering over the surface on a weedless hook or fishing on a weedless spoon. Yellow or Green are excellent. Red and White Pollywoggler also highly effective.

Pork Rind Eels—gaining in popularity as highly effective baits, especially for largemouth.

Bass Bugs

The fisherman should have a few of each major type: popping bugs, torpedo bugs, slim bugs, hoppers, frogs, mice, rubber legs, rubber skirt, weedless, deer-hair bugs, Henshall lures, mice, frogs, hoppers, keel bass bugs. Get a variety of colors and sizes as well as type.

The following offers an excellent, varied, and effective assortment.

Hard Body (Cork, Plastic)

Bar Cat, Weedless, #1 hook, White-green-yellow-gray (Falls)
Dylite Creepy Popperakle, #2, #4, Red and White, Yellow and Black (Weber)
Dylite Popping Frog, #4 (Weber)
Fish Head, #6, Black and White (Falls)
Fly Rod Hula Popper, 1/24 oz., Black (Fred Arbogast)
Long-Tom Popper, #8, Yellow (Glen Evans)
Marathon Grasshopper Fly, #4 (Marathon)

Deer Hair Bugs

Fly Rod Frog, #1/0 (Weber)
Hair Bug, #2, Natural (Phillips)
Hair Mouse, #4 (Orvis)
Henshall Lure, #2, Red-black and Red-black and white pattern (Weber)
Keel Fly Bass Bug, #2, Yellow Variant or Green Frog (Keel Fly Co.)
Marathon Bass Houn, #6, Gray-black-white (Marathon)
Marathon Croaker, #8, Green and Yellow (Marathon)

Flies

Dry Flies—Muddler Minnow, #4, Natural Wulff Flies, #6, Black, Brown, Gray, Royal

Streamer Flies—Black and White Bucktail, Black and Yellow Bucktail, Black-nosed Dace, Gov. Aiken, Gray Ghost, Grizzly King, Mickey Finn, Parmacheene Belle, Professor, Red and White Bucktail, Royal Coachman Bucktail, White Maribou, Yellow Maribou, and Yellow Perch. Sizes 1/0–4.

Don't neglect streamers; they are one of the finest, most effective bass lures. For use with spinners use H. O. B. Streamer Flies (Weber) or Multi-wing Streamers (Dan Bailey or Phillips) in bright patterns (Yellows, Reds, Whites, Oranges).

PIKE, PICKEREL, MUSKELLUNGE, WALLEYES AND SAUGER

Pike, pickerel, and muskellunge are members of the Pike family while walleyes and sauger are members of the Perch family. All are warm-water gamefish, preferring warmer water than trout and salmon, but still cooler water than bass, another warm-water fish. Actually, 60–65 degrees is the preferred temperature of pike, pickerel, muskies, walleyes, and sauger, whereas bass prefer 70–75 degrees. The fisherman needs to take water temperature into consideration in selecting lures and fishing methods for different times of the year. Shallow-water fishing is in order in the spring, fall, and until the water temperatures approach 65–70 degrees, but deeper water fishing is required during the warmer summer months.

PIKE

Plugs

The fisherman should select a small assortment of sizes, actions, and colors, but especially plugs which run at different depths. Pike are not nearly as fussy as bass, but the lures must be fished where the pike are: at depths of anywhere from the surface to 35 or 40 feet. Generally, floating-diving lures, or medium-depth lures are best in spring and fall (after the water has warmed above 55 degrees in the spring and cooled to 65 degrees in the fall). There is one exception: surface lures are excellent in the cooler water of fall, especially in the hour or so before dark. When the water warms to 70 degrees and over, the fisherman will have to go deeper with live bait or deep-running plugs. Studies have shown that plugs that are long and slim will catch more pike than short fat ones. Larger plugs catch fewer, but larger, pike. However, medium-size plugs (3 to 5 inches), will catch all sizes of pike, so don't use too large a plug unless you're fishing only for large pike.

Surface Plugs

Wounded minnow, torpedo-type lures are usually best.

Ballerina, (Torpedo type), ⅝ oz., Silver (Pflueger)
Dying Flutter (Spinners front and rear), Bullfrog (Daisy-Heddon)
L & S Mirrolure (Wounded Minnow Type), 5M Series, ½ oz., Red Head (L & S Bait Co.)

A few other surface lures add variety.

Crazy Crawler, ¼ oz., Gray Mouse (Daisy-Heddon)
Jitterbug, ⅝ oz., Frog/White Belly (Fred Arbogast)
Rebel Chuggerflash, ⅜ oz., Red Back (Norman)
Sputterbug, ¼ oz., Perch (Fred Arbogast)
Stick, ⅜ oz., Silver Back/Yellow Belly (Bomber)

Floating-Diving Plugs

Creek Chub Pike Minnow, ½ oz., Pikie (Creek Chub)
Flatfish, 3¾", Frog (Helin)
Hellcat, ½ oz., Black Back/Silver Scale (Whopper Stopper)
Rogue, ⅓ oz., Perch (Jack Smithwick)

Floating-Diving Deep-Diver Plugs

Deep Dive Tiger, ⅜ oz., Red Head (Daisy-Heddon)
Rebel, Deep Runner Minnow, ½ oz., Gold (Norman)

Sinking Plugs—Deep Divers

Deep River Runt Spook, ½ oz., Coach Dog (Daisy-Heddon)
Devil's Horse, Deep Runner, ½ oz., Silver Minnow (Jack Smithwick)
Tadpolly, ½ oz., Spotted Orange (Daisy-Heddon)

Sinking Plugs—Wobblers

L & S Pike Master, ⅝ oz., White body-Green back-Speckles (L & S Bait Co.)
Lazy Ike, ⅓ oz., Perch (Lazy Ike Corp.)
Rapala, 4⅜", Silver (Normark Corp)

Spoons

Spoons are probably the favorite lure for pike. The appeal is enhanced even further if a pork-rind strip is added.

Abu-Toby, ⅝ oz., Silver/Red (Garcia)
Good Luck Wobbler, 3⅝", Fluor. Red (H & J)
Johnson's Bucktail Spoon, ½ oz., Gold finish/Yellow Bucktail (Louis Johnson)
Marathon Rattle Spoon, ⅜ oz., Red and White/Copper (Marathon)
Red Eye Wiggler, Junior, ½ oz., Chrome (Hofschneider)
Skitter Spoon, ⅜ oz., Silver (John J. Hildebrandt) Use with pork rind.
Weber Spoons, Magnum (heavy metal), ⅜ oz., Hammered copper (Weber)
Williams Wobblers, ¾ oz., Half and half (Gold and Silver Mirrow) (William Gold Refining Co.)

Jigging Spoons

For summer or ice fishing. Even in the summer, pike sometimes like a spoon fluttering to the bottom. The Red Eye Wiggler, Weber Spoon, and Williams Wobbler listed above are excellent for this purpose. In addition, the following two jig spoons ought to be considered:

Laker Spoons, Russian Hook, #2 hook, Brass (Best Tackle)
Vi-ke, ½ oz., Nickel (Bridgeport Silver)

Spinners

Excellent, especially for deep-water trolling.

Marathon Big Slim, Natural, #4/0 hook (Marathon)
Marathon Fish Houn, 1/0 hook, Red and White (Marathon)
Mepps Giant Killer, 1½ oz., With Mino, Fluor. Red Blade (Sheldon's)
Pike Fin, ¾ oz., Black and Yellow (Worth)
Sabre Tooth Spinner, ¼ oz., Silver/White Head and Tail (Daisy-Heddon)
Tandem Spinner, 1/0 hook (Pflueger)
Weedless Wicked Willow, ⅜ oz., Nickel Spinner/Black and White Skirt (John J. Hildebrandt)

Bait

Bait is usually far better than lures from ice out until the water warms to 55 degrees. After that, lures are better until the fish go quite deep.

Frozen Smelt—4″ to 6″ long. The favorite ice fishing bait and best from ice out until the water warms to about 50°.
Live Minnows, Suckers—Best bet in the spring when water is from about 50°–60°, but good all of the time. Also good for deep water fishing in the hot summer months.
Frogs—A fine pike bait.
Cut Perch Belly—Good trolling rig/spinners.
Pork Rind—Use strips on spoons, spinners; use chunks on spoons, plain hooks.

Flies

Although flies are not often used for pike, they are excellent when the fish are in shallow water. Select a few large bass bugs for surface fishing (in the evening especially) and some large streamers for casting and trolling.

Bugs

Bugger, 1/0, Yellow (Falls)
Dylite Popping Frog, #2 (Weber)
Hair Mouse, #2 (Phillips)
Marathon Hair Frog, #1 (Marathon)

Streamer Flies

Select from blonde bucktail flies (Dan Bailey, Phillips), Universal Fly (Phillips), Mylar Body Bucktail Streamer Flies (Dan Bailey), or Multi-wing Streamers (Dan Bailey, Phillips, or Weber). See the chapter on Streamer Flies. Sizes 3/0–1/0.

PICKEREL

When the water temperature is comfortable (60–65 degrees is ideal) pickerel prefer the shallow weed-beds, undercut banks, bushes, logs, stumps, and other cover in shallow bays and inlets. Thus, from ice out until the water gets to over 65 degrees, you need lures which you can use in shallow water. After that, you'll have to go to the deep underwater beds until the water cools again in the fall, at which time pickerel move back to the shallows. Of course, during cloudy, cool weather, you may find some pickerel in the shallows during the summer months, but let the water get too warm and the larger fish have retreated to the deeper beds.

When in the shallows, pickerel love surface lures skittering over the surface. When deep, they will take jig crawlers, eels or other nature lures almost as readily as bass. They are a favorite ice fishing species also. Always hungry, they provide excellent sport year-round.

Plugs

Surface Lures

Wounded minnow plugs are by far the best, but any plug skittered over the surface is excellent.

Skip-N-Cisco, ¼ oz., Shiner Finish (Cisco Kid Tackle)
Sputterfuss, ¼ oz., Frog (Fred Arbogast)

Floating-Diving (Darters, Deep Divers, and Wobblers)

Creek Chub Darter, ⅜ oz., Pikie (Creek Chub)
Creek Chub Mouse, ¼ oz., Tiger (Creek Chub)
Rebel, Deep Runner Minnow, ⅜ oz., Silver (Norman)
Tiny River Runt Spook, ¼ oz., Perch (Daisy-Heddon)

Sinking Plugs (Deep Divers, Wobblers)

Cisco Kid Diver, ½ oz., Red and White (Cisco Kid)
Diamond Jim, ¼ oz., Gold Scale Minnow (Al's Goldfish Lure Co.)
Rapala, 3½", Silver (Normark)
Tadpolly, ½ oz., Bullfrog (Daisy-Heddon)

Spoons

Essentially all one needs is one red-and-white spoon with treble hook and one weedless (to which you should attach a pork strip).

Dardevle Spinnie, ¼ oz., Red and White/Nickel (Lou Eppinger)
Johnson's Silver Minnow, ¼ oz., Gold (Louis Johnson)

Spinners

Any type of propeller or fluted spinner to which is attached a weedless hook baited with a nightcrawler, minnow, frog, or pork rind is excellent skittered over the surface. Any type of weighted spinner lure is also excellent.

Herb's Dilly, ¼ oz., Frog and Yellow (Glen Evans)
Mepps Comet, ⅕ oz., Plain or with Mino (Sheldon's, Inc.)
Shyster, ¼ oz., Feathered, Brass Blade, Yellow and Black Spotted (Glen Evans)
Tony Accetta Hobo, ½ oz., Red Feather (Tony Accetta)

The Dilly and Hobo lures may be skittered over weeds, or fished deep.

Nature Lures

Frog

Jig and eel, or *jig and nightcrawler* are both excellent.

Bait

Frogs—Excellent summer bait especially; fish off bottom.

Minnows—About 3″ to 4″ long, good summer and through the ice.

Perch Belly—Cut strip used with weedless hook and spinner, skittered over the surface is excellent.

Uncle Josh Pork Frog—¼ oz. Green or Yellow. Use on weedless hook, skitter over weeds. One of the very best lures for pickerel. (Uncle Josh Bait Co.)

Flies

Same selection of bass bugs and streamers as for pike, or same streamers as recommended for bass.

MUSKELLUNGE

Musky will take surface lures readily, as well as other traditional, but large, floating-diving or sinking lures and wobbling spoons. They also like spinners and bucktails, trolled or cast. A live sucker is the favorite live bait.

Plugs

Surface Lures

Boy Howdy, 5/8 oz., Silver, spinners front and rear (Cordell)
Crazy Crawler, 5/8 oz., Bullfrog (Daisy-Heddon)
Musky Jitterbug, 1¼ oz., Perch (Fred Arbogast)

Floating-Diving Lures (Wobblers, Deep Divers)

Bass-Oreno, 5/8 oz., Red and White (Gladding-South Bend)
Bomber, ¾ oz., White/Black Shadows (Bomber Bait Co.)
Hellbender, 5/8 oz., Pink Eye Ghost (Whopper Stopper)
Mustang, 1½ oz., Green Back and Silver (Pflueger)
Pikie Minnow, 1 oz., Perch (Creek Chub)

Sinking Plugs (Deep Divers, Wobblers)

Husky Cisco Kid, 1¼ oz., Shad (Cisco Kid)
L & S Pike-Master, 5/8 oz., Yellow Belly-Brown Back-Speckles (L & S Bait Co.)
Rapala Magnum, 7″, Silver (Normark)

Spoons

Dardevle, 1 oz., Red and White/Nickel (Lou Eppinger)
Geneva Spoon, 3″, Chrome, Single Hook, for jigging (Arthur Freer)
Little Bantam, 1 oz., Hammered Brass (Southern Tool and Die Co.)
Red Eye Wiggler, 1 oz., Red and White, S-Stripe (Hofschneider)
Tony Accetta Pet Spoon, ¾ oz., Feather, Weedless, Red Feather (Tony Accetta)
Williams Weedless, 5/8 oz. Half and Half (Gold and Silver Mirror) (Williams Gold Refining Co.)

Spinners

Blackstone Musky Spinner, 7/8 oz., Silver Blade/Black Hair (S. R. Blackstone)
Marathon Musky Hawk, #4/0 hook, Natural (Marathon)
Marathon Musky Houn, #5/0 Weedless Treble, Red and White (Marathon)
Mepps Giant Killer, 1½ oz., With Mino, Gold/Red Dots Blade (Sheldon's)
Musky Tiger, 1 oz., Abalone Blade, Yellow (Worth)
Shannon Twin Spinner, 5/8 oz., Red (Shannon Lure Co.)
Weedless Musky King, 1 oz., Black and White (Weber)

Bait

Live suckers, 9″–12″ long. Trolled or cast with harness.
Mudpuppy (Salamander)

WALLEYES AND SAUGER

Several facts about walleyes and sauger will help the fisherman select his lures or bait.

1. Spawning takes place in water of temperature from 40–50 degrees. Thus, after ice out until the water reaches 50 degrees, you will find these fish in fairly shallow water over rocky, gravel bottoms where they spawn.

2. Walleyes have light-sensitive eyes, so they move back and forth from deep to shallow areas. A sunny day in clear water demands that you fish deep. On dark days, in turbid water, or at night, you can find them shallow if the water is fairly comfortable (60–65 degrees).

3. Walleyes like a very slow-moving lure or bait, bounced off the bottom.

4. They travel in schools, and are constantly wandering around. They frequently are caught over 100 miles from where tagged in rivers.

Plugs

Walleyes and sauger do not take surface lures readily, preferring underwater lures fished along the bottom at whatever depths they are feeding. The fisherman needs a small assortment of floating-diving, sinking, and deep-diving plugs in reasonably small sizes.

Floating Diving Plugs (Deep Divers and Wobblers)

Bomber, ½ oz., Green Shad (Bomber)
Hellbender, ¼ oz., Yellow Perch (Whopper Stopper)
Huncho, ¼ oz., Red Head (Cordell)
Little Big Dig, Black Dace (Burke)
Rebel, Deep-Runner Minnow, ¼ oz., Silver (Norman)
ThinFin Super Shiner Minnow, ⅛ oz., Purple (Storm)

Sinking Plugs (Deep Divers, Vibrators, Wobblers)

Flatfish, 3″, Lt. Underwater, White, Red Head, Black Top (Helin)
Rapala, 2¾″, Blue (Normark)
Sonic, ⅜ oz., Yellow (Daisy-Heddon)
Tiny Tad, ¼ oz., Bullfrog (Daisy-Heddon)

Jigs

Jigs are one of the favorite lures for walleyes and sauger. Get an assortment, sizes ⅛–½ ounce in the following colors: yellow, white, black, red, blue, or combinations of these; black and white, red and white, blue and white, black and yellow.

See the section on Jigs and Jig Combinations.

Spinners

Spinners are most frequently used in combination with live bait. The June Bug Spinner, Colorado Spinner, or Indiana Spinner are favorites, attached to a minnow, frog, or nightcrawler in a harness. The Colorado Spinner with a plain treble hook and nightcrawler is frequently used. Spinners are also used as part of deep-trolling rigs, usually with live bait. A spinner and fly combination is also effective.

Weighted Spinners are also used some. The following are popular.

Abu-Reflex, 1/4 oz., Yellow body/Chrome Blade (Garcia)
Mepps Aglia, 1/6 oz., Black And White/Gray Squirrel Tail (Sheldon's)
Paul Bunyan "66", 1/4 oz., Red and White (Prescott)
Shyster, 1/8 oz., Brass blade/Yellow and Black Spotted Body (Glen Evans)

Spoons

Deep-running spoons are excellent, especially those that can be fished slowly with a maximum of action. This means broad-shaped wobblers.

Dardevle Spinnie, 1/4 oz., Black and White Stripe/Brass (Lou Eppinger)
Lake Clear Wobbler, 2", Copper. Use a treble hook for trolling, a single hook for jigging, a snelled hook for live bait, or 2 snelled hooks for live bait. Buy several to get different rigs. (Arthur Freer)
Red Flash Wobbler, 1/4 oz., Chrome (Horrocks-Ibbotson)
Worth Casting Spoon, Heavyweight, 1/4 oz., Red and White/Nickel (Worth)

Jigging spoons are also helpful, especially through the ice, baited with a fish eye, minnow or nightcrawler.

Geneva Spoon, 2", Chrome, Single Hook (Arthur Freer)
Johnson's Lucky Lujon, 3/8 oz., Brass, Treble Hook (Louis Johnson)
Lake Clear Wobbler (See above)
Saginaw Bay Jig Spoon, 1 5/8 oz., Plain single hook (Best Tackle)
Swedish Jig, 1/8 oz., Single hook, Nickel (Best Tackle)

Bait

Minnows—Live, 2″ to 3″ long, for still fishing, drift fishing. A dead minnow (but fresh) in a harness will work trolling, or deep-water casting. Shiners are probably most popular, followed by chubs. Live minnows are also the most popular ice fishing bait. For trolling, sew on the minnow or use a small harness. Threadfin shad and herring minnows are used locally in a few states.

Nightcrawlers, worms are the second choice among live bait options. These are most often used on a nightcrawler rig, or with a spinner. A worm or nightcrawler on a Mepps-type weighted spinner, or on a Colorado spinner, with treble hooks, is excellent fished very slowly just off the bottom.

Frogs are a favorite where laws forbid using minnows. May be fished with a spinner just off the bottom, trolling or drift fishing, or on bottom still fishing.

Hellgrammites and small *crawfish* are used some, but are more effective in rivers than in lakes.

Pork rind in strips, fished on a spoon, fly, or spinner is a very effective lure for walleyes. Try green, yellow, white, black, red.

PANFISH

The fish included in this chapter are from three major families of freshwater fish.

Sunfish Family—Bluegill, crappie, rock bass, warmouth bass, and other sunfish (green orange-spotted, redear or shellcracker, pumpkin seed, longear, redbreast, spotted or stumpknocker, and Sacramento perch).

Sea-Bass Family—White bass, yellow bass, white perch.

Perch Family—Yellow perch.

Before recommending specific lures, flies, and bait, it would be well to discuss a few basic characteristics and habits of these fish which affect the selection of lures, flies, and bait.

Sunfish Family

Sunfishes might be subdivided into three groups: bluegill and other true sunfish, crappie (both black and white crappie), and rock and warmouth bass. All of them spawn in the spring as the water temperature approaches 65–70 degrees. They stay in fairly shallow water until the temperature gets between 70–75 degrees and then they gradually retire to deeper water, 6–20 feet deep, for the warmer summer months. Early morning, evening and night, however, they will often move to the shallows to feed. As the water begins cooling off in the fall below the 70–75 degree range, the fish move back into shallower water, or occupy any water where there is feed. After the water cools to 65 degrees and below, the fish move back to deeper water (10–15 feet) and become less active.

The *bluegill* and *other true sunfishes* primarily feed on crustaceans, plants and insects. The adults eat crustaceans, vegetation, larvae, nymphs, and adult insects. Only occasionally do they eat small fish or fish eggs. This means they are caught primarily on selected types of live bait (nymphs, larvae, insects, worms), nature lures, and artificial flies and nymphs. All of these sunfish, except redears or shellcrackers, respond readily to artificial flies. Shellcrackers seem to confine their diet to snails and other crustaceans. Sunfish all have small mouths, which means bait or fly hook sizes must be small.

They feed on larger mouthfuls during the warm summer months, but are very delicate eaters of small foods in the winter. Ice fishing lures or bait must be very small and delicate.

Crappie (both black and white) have fairly large, although delicate, mouths. This means baits and lures may be larger than for bluegill and other sunfish, although once hooked the fish must be handled carefully. Crappie do best in large rivers or lakes where there is plenty of room to move about after the forage fish which is their staple diet. They like tangled brush, stumps, weedbeds, and other such cover for their resting places. However, because they move about in schools to forage, the fisherman will find them in different places on different days. And, because adult crappie like to feed on forage fish, they can be caught readily on small spinners, spoons, jigs, plugs, and flyrod streamers and lures, all of which represent small fish. They do eat some insect nymphs, larvae and adults, primarily early in the season, and so can sometimes be caught on regular flies and nymphs, but generally, imitations representing small fish are best. For live bait, minnows 1 to 2 inches long are the favorite.

Rock bass and *warmouth bass* eat everything and can be caught on everything. They have a good-sized mouth and will strike most any kind of bait or artificial when in the mood. They hit plugs, spoons, spinners, flies, or a variety of live baits with equal abandon. Thus, they can be caught spinning, fly fishing, or bait fishing.

Sea-Bass Family

Members of this family include: *white bass, yellow bass,* and *white perch*. All are members of this same family of fish as are striped bass in the ocean. These fish are all forage fish, moving determinedly about a lake in large schools as they follow baitfish. Therefore, they are caught primarily on lures, flies, and bait representing small fishes. However, since they also eat insects, larvae, and nymphs, they can also be caught on dry and wet flies and nymphs (these are poorer attractors than minnow-type flies and lures).

In early spring they move up rivers and streams to spawn and can be readily caught in these places during this time of year. In the heat of summer they may be 30 to 50 feet deep, or (especially early morning and late evening or night) roaming the surface looking for food. They are superb fighting fish and may be caught with spinning, fly fishing, or live-bait gear.

Perch Family

Yellow perch is the only panfish discussed in this chapter which belongs to the true Perch family. It is also a forage fish, moving about a lake in schools of from 50 to 200 fish. The schools are stratified by size and age of fish. Yellow perch are primarily meat eaters. Their gill rakers enable them to strain out small organisms from the water. The stomachs of small perch are ordinarily filled with microscopic crustaceans and midge larvae. Adults eat large numbers of larger larvae, nymphs, crustacea (such as crawfish), and various baitfish. Because of their varied diet, they respond well to a variety of spinning and fly fishing lures and techniques and to numerous live baits. However, except for a brief period in the spring during spawning activity, yellow perch (especially the larger fish) like fairly deep water (up to 50 feet deep). You can always catch small perch in the shallow weed beds, but the larger fish are caught in deeper water. Thus, spinning, trolling, or bait fishing is easier for these deep-water fish than is fly fishing. Also, the schools of yellow perch dispense at night and the fish rest quietly along the bottom nearer shore. Thus, they are daytime feeders and cannot be caught at night.

Plugs for Panfish

Plugs are most suitable for those panfish which eat quantities of small fish. This group includes crappie, rock and warmouth bass, white and yellow bass, white perch, and yellow perch.

A good assortment should include plugs of a variety of actions, sizes, and colors, and which run at various depths. Most should be small because the size of the fish caught is small.

Surface Lures

Baby Crippled Killer, 1/8 oz., Yellow Perch (Phillips)
Creek Chub Injured Minnow, 1/8 oz., Red and White (Creek Chub)
Creek Chub Plunker, 1/8 oz., Pikie (Creek Chub)
Jitterbug, 1/8 oz, Frog/White Belly (Fred Arbogast)
Rebel Poppers, 1/8 oz., Silver (Norman)
Weighted Spin Popper, 1/8 oz., Black Belly/Yellow stripes (Glen Evans)

The addition of a small dry fly, panfish bug, or wet fly, attached with a nylon trailer to the plug, will catch fish with small mouths that are striking but not getting hooked.

Floating-Diving Lures (Darters, Wobblers, Deep Divers)

Creek Chub Darter, 1/8 oz., Frog (Creek Chub)
Creek Chub Pikie Minnow, 1/8 oz., Perch (Creek Chub)
Finn-Oreno, 3/16 oz. (3½″), Silver Back (Gladding-South Bend)
Flatfish, 1¾″ and 2½″, Frog or White/Assorted spots (Helin)
Rainbow Runner, 1/8 oz., Gold fish (Phillips)
Rapala, 2″, Blue (Normark)

Rascal, ¼ oz., (1¾"), Yellow (Gladding-South Bend)
Rebel, Deep-Runner Minnow, ⅛ oz; Red Back (Norman)
Rebel, Shiner Minnow, 1/16 oz., Fluor. Red (Norman)
ThinFin Super Shiner Minnow, ⅛ oz., (2½"), Green (Norman)
Tiny Lucky 13, ¼ oz., Golden Shiner (Daisy-Heddon)
Tiny River Runt Spook, ¼ oz., Red Head/Flitter (Daisy-Heddon)

Sinking Lures (Deep Divers, Vibrators, Wobblers)

Deep Inch, ¼ oz., Black Dace (Falls Bait Co.)
Harrison's Rocky Lure: Junior—1/16 oz. (1"), Red and White; Senior—⅛ oz. (1½"), Yellow/Black Dots (Harrison-Hoge)
Inch Minnow, 1/16 oz., Orange Tiger, or Pearl Spot (Falls)
L & S Mirrolures (Jointed), 1/16 oz., Green back-white belly-silver scale (L & S Bait Co.)
L & S Spin-Master, 1/16 oz., Yellow body/brown bars (L & S)
L & S Mirrolure (Trail-O-Lure), 1/16 oz., Silver (L & S)
Rapala, 2", Silver (Normark)
Tiny Ike, ¼ oz., Black-White Shore (Daisy-Heddon)
Ultra-Sonic, ⅛ oz., Coach Dog (Daisy-Heddon)

Spoons For Panfish

Spoons are primarily for fish-eating panfish.

Al's Goldfish, 3/16 oz., Gold (Al's Goldfish Lure Co.)
Dardevle, Skeeter Plus: 2/32 oz. Red and White/Nickel
Lil' Devle: ⅛ oz.
Midget: 3/16 oz.
Demon Spoon, 1/32 oz., Nickel (Worth)
Feathered Shad-King, #2, White Hackle (Hildebrandt)
Gemini Spoon, 1/30 oz., Gold (Al's Goldfish)
Johnson's Bucktail Spoon, ½ oz., Black Nickel/Black and white Bucktail (Louis Johnson)
Johnson's Sprite, ⅛ oz., Blue Mullet (Louis Johnson)
K-B Spoon, 1/16 oz., Copper (Prescott)
Little Bantam, ¼ oz., Hammered Brass (Southern Tool & Die Co.)
Little Cleo, ⅛ oz., Black and yellow (Seneca)

Marathon Dictator, 1/8 oz., Black and White Stripe/Nickel (Marathon)
Midge, 1/24 oz., Brass (Glen Evans)
Phantom Wobbler, Baby, Pearl/copper (H & J)
Slim Spoon, 1/8 oz., Hammered Nickel (Weber)
Super Duper, 1/6 oz., Red Head (Gladding-South Bend)
Tony Accetta Pet Spoon, 1/16 oz., Standard Model, Feathered, Gold/Red Feather (Tony Accetta)
Williams Nymphs, 1/40 oz. (1¼"), Silver Mirror (Williams)

Jigging Spoons

Select from Mitzi Series, Russian Hooks (Jig Spoons), Tear Drop Series (Best Tackle Mfg. Co.) described in chapter on Spoons. For use in ice fishing.

Spinners For Panfish

For all kinds of panfish. Any type of spinner with a snelled hook and bait makes an excellent casting or trolling lure for panfish. Use larger spinners for trolling than casting. See the section on Spinners. Spinner and fly, or spinner and pork rind are also excellent.

Weighted Spinners

Abu-Reflex, 1/16 oz., Yellow/Black Dots (Garcia)
Colorado Spinner, 3/0 blade, Nickel (Glen Evans)
Droppen, 1/8 oz., Gold (Garcia)
Flicker-Spinner, #2, Nickel (Hildebrandt)
Hep, 1/8 oz., Silver, Squirrel Tail (Daisy-Heddon)
Little Fooler, 1/12 oz., Red and White Skirt (Hildebrandt)
Marathon Bream Buster, 1/8 oz., Black and Yellow (Marathon)
Marathon Spin-O-Hawk, 1/8 oz., Black and Yellow (Marathon)
Mepps Aglia, 1/8 oz., Red and White Spinner Blade, Bare Treble Hook (Sheldon's)
Mepps Black Fury, 1/8 oz., Yellow hair (Sheldon's)
Panther Martin, Regular, 1/16 oz., Silver Blade/Yellow and Red Body (Harrison-Hoge)

Worden's Rooster Tail, $\frac{1}{16}$ oz., Flame (Yakima)
Worth Pearlie, $\frac{1}{6}$ oz. (Worth)
Worth Scamp, $\frac{1}{8}$ oz. White/Black Dots (Worth)

Jigs for Panfish

Jigs are one of the finest lures for crappie. They are also excellent for white and yellow bass and are used to some extent on yellow perch. Get an assortment of types, sizes, and colors. White, yellow, pink are favorite colors. Blue, red, fluor. orange, red, or pink, black, and combinations of these (red and white, black and white, pink and white, blue and white, black and yellow, red and yellow, or white and yellow) are used to some extent. Buy sizes $\frac{1}{32}$–$\frac{1}{4}$ ounce. (The larger jigs are used on occasion with white and yellow bass particularly.) The following offers a good assortment:

Baby Lead Head Jig, #6 hook, Fluor. Red and White (Glen Evans)
BJ Bucktail Jig, $\frac{1}{8}$ oz., All White. Shaped Bucktail Jig (Banana Head), $\frac{1}{16}$ oz., All Yellow (Horrocks-Ibbotson)
Crappie Killer, #10 hook, Fluor. Red and White (Weber)
Fin-Nit, #8 hook, Black (Arndt & Sons)
Full Tail Jig, $\frac{1}{32}$ oz., White (Assassinator Lures)
Hot-Line, $\frac{1}{32}$ oz., Pearl (Arndt & Sons)
Jig Ike, $\frac{1}{16}$ oz., Black (Lazy Ike Corp.)
Li'l Crappie Killer, $\frac{1}{16}$ oz., Silver and Blue (Cordell)
Little Doggie Maribou Jig Fly, $\frac{1}{32}$ oz., Yellow/Black and Yellow (Glen Evans)
Little-Hornet Jig Fly, $\frac{1}{32}$ oz., Mud Dauber Finish (Arndt & Sons)
Marathon Canadian Minnow, $\frac{1}{16}$ oz., Black and White (Marathon)
Pinkie Jig, $\frac{1}{4}$ oz. White (Marathon)
Panfish Weighted Hair Fly, #8, Fluor. Pink/White Tail (Glen Evans)
Plain Jig Head, $\frac{1}{32}$ oz., $\frac{1}{16}$ oz., $\frac{1}{8}$ oz. Use with live bait, pork strip (Assassinator Lures)
Worth Ball Head Jig, $\frac{1}{8}$ oz., White and Yellow, or Black and White, or Yellow feather streamers (Worth)

Ice Fishing Jig Spoons, Flies

These are used for all types of panfish, especially with live bait. See the previous section on jigging spoons.

Nature Lures For Panfish

By far the best all-round nature lure for panfish is the plastic worm, trolled or cast, and used on a small, two-hook spinner rig. Use a worm, natural or red, 2 to 3 inches long. My favorite rig is the No. FR–432 Panfish Worm Lure, 2⅜-inch plastic worm, with two #7 hooks and Colorado Spinner, by Sportsman's Products. (The reason I like it is the trailer hook is right on the end of the worm, readily catching any panfish which bites the tail. If the fisherman threads his own, he should put the hook near the tail.) Burke Flexo-Products also sells a 2½-inch worm on a two-hook rig with nylon shaft and aerospinner. Delong sells a 1⅞-inch tiny plastic worm with two hooks molded into the worm (no spinner). Falls Bait Co. sells a 2- or 2½-inch worm and rig with two #10 gold hooks, nylon shaft and propeller spinner.

In addition to worms, I would buy the following nature lures.

Crawfish: Primarily for rock and warmouth bass, yellow perch.

Flyrod Size, #10 hook (Burke Flexo-Products Co.)
Small, single hook (Creme Lure Co.)

Frogs: Primarily for rock and warmouth bass, yellow perch.

Flyrod Frog, 1½", Brown or Green (Burke)
Brown Frog, or Green Frog, Small (#10) (Creme)

Insects: For most panfish, especially the insect eaters.

Caddis Fly: #12, Brown or Yellow (Creme)
Cricket: Black, #10 (Creme Lures)
Black Floating Cricket, #8 (Burke)
Tru-Life Cricket, #8, Black (Weber)
Grasshopper: Green or Yellow Grasshopper, Small #10 (Creme)
Brown (Burke)
Tru-Life Grasshopper, #10 (Weber)
Spider: Floating Panfish Spider, Orange and Black, #8 (Burke)
Stone Fly: #10 (Creme)

Larvae: For most panfish, especially the insect eaters.

Babby Hellgrammite, #10 (Burke)
Caddis Worm, #12 (Creme Lure)
Catalpa Worm, Small (Creme)
Grub Worm (Midwest Tackle)
Mayfly Nymph, #8 (Burke) Also, Tru-Life May Nymph (Weber)
Stonefly Nymph, #10 (Burke)

Minnows: Especially for fish-eating panfish.

Life Like Lures, Minnows, 1¾″ or 2¾″, soft. Black and Silver, Gray (3-L Products)
Spinner Minnow, 2″ or 3″, Shiner (Weber)
Tiny Flash Minnow, (1¼″), or Jr. Flash Minnow (2″) with propeller spinner (Delong Lures)

Artificial Bugs and Flies

Panfish Bugs (Floating)

Band-It Popper, #8, Yellow and Black (Glen Evans)
Dylite Deluxe Creepy Popper, #10 Black and White (Weber)
Dylite Zebra Popper, #12, Black/Yellow Stripes (Weber)
Fire Fly Shimmy, #10, Fire Orange (Falls Bait Co.)
Firelure Nitwit, #12, Green Frog (Weber)
Half-Wit, #16, Black (Weber)
Marathon Grasshopper Fly, #8, 12, 16 (Marathon)

Mountain (deer hair) Hopper, #10 (Phillips)
Ruf-Rubber: Waterbug—#10, Varmint—#10, Skip-It—#10 — Black, Yellow, Buff, Green colors (Glen Evans)
Screwball, #14, Red and White, or Yellow (Glen Evans)
Sizzler, #10, Yellow (Falls)
Water-Waif, #10, Black (Glen Evans)
Wisp, #8, Green-black-gray (Falls)

Dry Flies

Bivisible: Black, Brown, Gray, Grizzly—#8
Divided Wing: Adams, Black Gnat, Iron Blue Dun, Light Cahill, March Brown, Mosquito, Pink Lady, White Miller—#10, 12
Fanwing: Royal Coachman—#12
Gauze Wing: Gauze Wing Drake (Blue Dun, Yellow, Ginger), #12 (Phillips)
Hackle: Brown Hackle Yellow, Gray Hackle Red—#10
Hairbody: Goofus Bug (#14—Yellow body) (Dan Bailey)
Irresistible, #10, Natural (Orvis)
Hairwing: Wulff Flies: Black, Blonde, Grizzly, Royal—#8, 14

Wet Flies

Divided Wing: Black Gnat, Coachman, Cowdung, Gold Ribbed Hare's Ear, McGinty, Montreal, Parmacheene Belle, Royal Coachman, Western Bee—#8, 12
Featherwing: Professor—#10
Wooly Worms: Green, Brown—#8, 12
Hairwing: Picket Pin (Squirrel tail, yellow body—#10)
Rubber Body, Legs: Fall's Spider, #10, Black, Yellow, Green
Bream Wiggler, #8, Black (Falls)
Panfish Flies: Marathon Red Tail Crappie Fly, #8 (Select desired patterns from description in chapter on Wet Flies.)
Weber Brim-Fli, #10, Black/White or Red Tail, or Yellow/Red Tail, or Gray/Red Tail. For use with spinner. (Weber)

Nymphs (Weighted)

Black and Yellow (Worth)
Caddis Fly (Dan Bailey)
Tan Shrimp (Dan Bailey)

Gray Nymph (Orvis)
Mayfly Nymph, Black, Brown, Tan, Yellow (Dan Bailey)
Ted's Stonefly Nymph, Black and Orange (Orvis)
Tellico (Orvis)
Sizes #10–14

Streamer Flies

Black and White Bucktail
Blacknosed Dace
Black Ghost
Edson Tiger Dark
Gray Ghost
Mickey Finn
Muddler (Natural)
Nine-Three
Parmacheene Belle
Professor
Red and White Bucktail
White Maribou
Yellow Maribou
#6–10

Terrestrials

Ants: Black, Red—#16
Grasshopper: Dan's Deer Hopper Fly—#12 (Dan Bailey)
Worth Special Hornberg Fly—#10 (Worth)
Jassid: Black, Orange, Yellow—#16 (Dan Bailey)

Bait For Panfish

Practically every type of live and dead bait have been used at one time or another for panfish. The following is a list of favorites.

Worms, Nightcrawlers—The universal favorite for all panfish.

Minnows—Excellent for fish-eating panfish: crappie, rock and warmouth bass, white and yellow bass, white perch, yellow perch.

Cockroaches, Crickets, Grasshoppers—Used for all types of panfish except white and yellow bass. Used most on bluegills and other true sunfish, especially in late, warm summer months.

Catalpa Worms—Useful for all panfish, especially for bluegills.

Gall Worms, Meal Worms, Maggots—Used most often as ice-fishing baits, especially for bluegills.

Grubs—For all panfish except white and yellow bass.

Caddis Worms, Damsel Fly Nymphs, Dragonfly Nymphs, Mayfly Nymphs, and *Stonefly Nymphs*—When obtainable are excellent for all panfish except white and yellow bass.

Crane-fly Larvae—Used primarily as ice-fishing bait for bluegills (they are called mousees).

Hellgrammites—Especially useful for rock and warmouth since they inhabit flowing water in streams.

Clams, Mussels—Small bites are excellent for bluegill, shellcrackers, other sunfish, and yellow perch.

Crawfish—Excellent, especially for rock bass, yellow perch. Will work on white and yellow bass, white perch.

Freshwater Shrimp—One of the principal food of white perch. Will work on all panfish.

Frogs—The only important amphibians useful for panfish. In small sizes they are excellent for yellow perch.

Cut Fish—Small pieces are excellent for rock and warmouth bass, yellow perch.

Fish Eyes—The eyes of yellow perch are one of the very best ice-fishing baits for yellow perch.

Salmon Eggs—All right for bluegills, sunfish, yellow perch, especially if jigged.

Pork Rind—Small strips attached to spinners, flies, spoons give added attraction. The very small frog pork chunk works well on yellow perch.

APPENDIX

Names and addresses of fishing tackle manufacturers of lures, flies, or bait described in this book.

Al's Goldfish Lure Co., 516 Main Street, Orchard, Massachusetts, 01051

Arndt and Sons, Inc., 1000 Fairview Ave., Hamilton, Ohio, 45015

The Arnold Tackle Co., Paw Paw, Michigan, 49079

Arthur T. Freer, Gilbertsville, New York, 13776

Assassinator Lures, 1405 Austin, Oak Grove, Missouri, 64075

Best Tackle Mfg. Co., 3106 Bay Street, Box 123, Unionville, Michigan, 48767

Bomber Bait Co., Box 106, Gainesville, Texas, 76240

Bridgeport Silverware Mfg. Corp., 65 Holland Ave., Bridgeport, Connecticut, 06605

Buck's Baits, Hickory, North Carolina

Burke Flexo-Products Co., Box 348, Traverse City, Michigan, 49684

Chev Chase Lures, Wilmott Flat, New Hampshire, 03287

Cisco Kid Tackle, 2630 N.W. 1st Ave., Boca Raton, Florida, 33432

Cordell Tackle, Inc., Box 2020, Hot Springs, Arkansas, 71901

Creek Chub Bait Co., 116 East Keyser Street, Garrett, Indiana, 46738

Creme Lure Company, Rt. #2, Box 16A, Tyler, Texas, 75701

Daisy-Heddon, Rogers, Arkansas, 72756
Dan Bailey Fly Shop, Box 1019, 209 West Park Street, Livingston, Montana, 59047
DeLong Lures, 85 Compark Road, Centerville, Ohio, 45459
Eddie Pope and Co., Inc., 25572 Avenue Stanford, Valencia, Calif., 91355
Falls Bait Co., Chippewa Falls, Wisconsin, 54729
Fred Arbogast Co., Inc., 313 West North Street, Akron, Ohio, 44303
Fred Doetzel, 19241 1st Ave. N.E., Cedar Rapids, Iowa, 52402
The Garcia Corp., 329 Alfred Ave., Teaneck, New Jersey, 07666
Gladding-South Bend Tackle, South Otselic, New York, 13155
Glen L. Evans, Inc., Caldwell, Idaho, 83605
H and J Fishing Tackle, NOrthboro, Mass., 01532
Hank Roberts Outfitters, Box 308, Boulder, Colorado, 80302
Harrison-Hoge Industries, 104 Arlington Ave., St. James Long Island, New York, 11780
Helin Tackle Co., 4068 Beaufait Avenue, Detroit, Michigan, 48207
Hofschneider Corp., Box 4166, Rochester, New York, 14611
Horrocks Ibbotson Co., 20 Whitesboro Street, Utica, New York, 13502
Jack K. Smithwick and Son, Box 1205, Shreveport, Louisiana, 71102
J.A. Greene, Inc., Boston Rd., Sutton, Mass., 01527
John J. Hildebrandt Corp., Logansport, Indiana, 46947
The Keel Fly Co., Box 2000, Traverse City, Michigan, 49684
L & S Bait Co., Bradley, Illinois, 60915
Lazy Ike Corp., Box 1177, Fort Dodge, Iowa, 50501

Louis Johnson Co., 1547 Old Deerfield Rd., Highland Park, Illinois, 60035

Lou J. Eppinger Mfg. Co., 6340 Schaefer Hwy., Dearborn, Michigan, 48126

Marathon Bait Co., 930 Single Ave., Wausau, Wisconsin, 54401

M. Behrens, 241 N. Kendrick Ave., Burlington, Wisconsin, 53105

Midwest Tackle, Box 10763, St. Louis, Missouri, 63129

Norman Manufacturing Co., Inc., 2910 Jenny Lind Road, Ft. Smith, Arkansas, 72901

Normark Corp., 1710 East 78th. St., Minneapolis, Minn., 55423

The Orvis Co., Manchester, Vermont, 05254

Otterget Lure Co., Box 123, Ashby, Mass., 01431

Pcola's Lures, Box 61, St. Michael, Pa., 15951

Pflueger Sporting Goods Division, Box 310, Hollandale, Florida, 33009

Phillips Fly and Tackle Co., Alexandria, Pennsylvania, 16611

Prescott Spinner Co., 313 W. North Street, Akron, Ohio, 44303

Seneca Tackle Co., Box 2841, Elmwood Station, Providence, Rhode Island, 02907

Shannon Lure Co., 3654 W. Montrose Ave., Chicago, Illinois, 60618

Sheldon's, Inc., Box 508, Antigo, Wisconsin, 54409

Southern Tool and Die Co., Box 5696, Asheville, North Carolina, 28803

Sportsman's Products, Inc., Box 37, Marion, Indiana, 46952

S.R. Blackstone, 403 Powers Ave., Madison, Wisconsin, 53714

Stembridge Products, Inc., Box 90756, 2941 Central Ave., East Point, Georgia, 30344

Storm Manufacturing Co., Box 265, Norman, Oklahoma, 73069

3-L Products Co., 717 Washington Street, Huntingdon, Pa., 16652

Tony Accetta and Son, Inc., 932 Avenue E., Riviera Beach, Florida, 33404

Uncle Josh Bait Co. 524 Clarence Street, Fort Atkinson, Wisconsin, 53538

Weber Tackle Co., Stevens Point, Wisconsin, 54481

Whopper Stopper, Inc., Box 1111, Sherman, Texas, 75090

Williams Gold Refining Co. of Canada, Ltd., 30 Courtwright Street, Fort. Erie, Ontario, Canada

The Worth Co., Box 88, Stevens Point, Wisconsin, 54481

Yakima Bait Co., Box 310, Granger, Washington, 98932